Dictionary of Money, Banking and Finance

Also from New Century

- Dictionary of Economics
- Dictionary of Public Finance
- Dictionary of Capital Market
- Dictionary of Marketing and Advertising
- Dictionary of Insurance
- Dictionary of International Trade and Business
- Encyclopaedia of Economics and Commerce (*in two volumes*)

Dictionary of

Money, Banking and Finance

(Including a Glossary of E-money and E-banking Terms)

By

Dr. Benson Kunjukunju
Associate Professor,
Post-graduate and Research Department of Commerce,
St. Thomas College, Kozhencherry, Kerala

New Century Publications
New Delhi, India

NEW CENTURY PUBLICATIONS
4800/24, Bharat Ram Road,
Ansari Road, Daryaganj,
New Delhi - 110 002 (India)

Tel.: 011-2324 7798, 4358 7398, 6539 6605
Fax: 011-4101 7798
E-mail: indiatax@vsnl.com • info@newcenturypublications.com
www.newcenturypublications.com

Editorial office:
LG–7, Aakarshan Bhawan,
4754-57/23, Ansari Road, Daryaganj,
New Delhi – 110 002

Tel.: 011-4356 0919

First Published: **July 2014**

ISBN: **978-81-7708-386-6**

Published by New Century Publications and printed at Salasar Imaging Systems, New Delhi.

Designs: Patch Creative Unit, New Delhi.

PRINTED IN INDIA

About the Dictionary

Money is the pivot around which a modern economy revolves. Finance is the life blood of business activities. Banking system, as an integral part of the financial sector, is the linchpin of any development strategy. Banking system, along with other constituents of the financial sector, helps to mobilise financial surpluses of an economy and transfers them to areas of financial deficit. It promotes savings by providing a wide variety of financial assets to the general public. Savings collected from the household sector are pooled together and allocated to various sectors of the economy for raising production levels. If the allocation of credit is judicious and socially equitable, it can help achieve the twin objectives of growth and social justice.

This dictionary is designed to provide a useful, reliable, readable and *single source* guide to the all-pervasive field of money, banking and finance. It provides simple and easily comprehensible definitions and explanations of terms used in these areas worldwide. The terms, concepts and usages are given their most common definition. Readers will also find helpful illustrations of important terms.

This reference work is intended as a practical tool for a cross-section of readership. It will be useful for teachers and students of economics, commerce, law, and management, and also for bankers, corporate executives, legislators and government officials. Meticulously cross-referenced, the dictionary is a comprehensive and invaluable source of essential information.

About the Author

Dr. Benson Kunjukunju is presently Associate Professor in the Post-graduate and Research Department of Commerce, St. Thomas College, Kozhencherry, under Mahatma Gandhi University, Kottayam, Kerala. He did his M.Com., M.Phil. and Ph.D. from the University of Kerala, Trivandrum. He has more than 30 years of teaching experience at undergraduate and post-graduate levels. He is a recognized research guide of the Faculty of Commerce, Mahatma Gandhi University, Kottayam.

Dr. Kunjukunju has published 4 books and a good number of research articles in national and international journals of repute. His areas of specialization include financial accounting, financial institutions and financial markets.

Contents

How Best to Use This Dictionary

Money is the pivot around which a modern economy revolves. Finance is the life blood of business activities. Banking system, as an integral part of the financial sector, is the linchpin of any development strategy. Banking system, along with other constituents of the financial sector, helps to mobilise financial surpluses of an economy and transfers them to areas of financial deficit. It promotes savings by providing a wide variety of financial assets to the general public. Savings collected from the household sector are pooled together and allocated to various sectors of the economy for raising production levels. If the allocation of credit is judicious and socially equitable, it can help achieve the twin objectives of growth and social justice.

This dictionary is designed to provide a useful, reliable, readable and *single source* guide to the all-pervasive field of money, banking and finance. It provides simple and easily comprehensible definitions and explanations of terms used in these areas worldwide. The terms, concepts and usages are given their most common definition. Readers will also find helpful illustrations of important terms.

This reference work is intended as a practical tool for a cross-section of readership. It will be useful for teachers and students of economics, commerce, law, and management, and also for bankers, corporate executives, legislators and government officials. Meticulously cross-referenced, the dictionary is a comprehensive and invaluable source of essential information.

The entries in the dictionary are arranged in strict alphabetical order, letter by letter. A complete list of entries is given on pages xv to xxxiv of the dictionary. All entries are followed by the page number at which they respectively appear.

To make the best use of the material included in the dictionary and also to avoid repetition, entries are elaborately and meticulously cross referenced in the following manner.

1. Cross-references immediately following an entry either indicate interchangeable terms—e.g. **Dirty Float** See Managed Float—or

direct the reader to the relevant description where that particular term is treated as part of a larger (essay type) entry, e.g. **Balance Sheet of a Commercial Bank** See Commercial Bank. Cross references are followed by the page number at which they appear.

2. Cross-references at the end of an entry point to the treatment of a related subject explained elsewhere in the dictionary, e.g. **Nostro Account:** Account of a bank in a foreign bank is called nostro account. For example, a Mumbai bank's dollar account in a New York bank is a nostro account. See also Vostro Account.
3. Terms which appear during description of another term and are followed by (q.v.*) are entered separately at relevant places in the dictionary, e.g. **Accrual Basis Accounting:** There are two main methods of accounting: accrual basis accounting and Cash Basis Accounting (q.v.).
4. A term with popular abbreviation/acronym is entered in expanded form as, for example, **Unit Trust of India (UTI).** However, abbreviation/acronym of a term also appears as a separate entry, though the reader is directed to the expanded form of the entry as, for example, **UTI:** See Unit Trust of India. Also, an abbreviation/acronym is entered in expanded form on its first appearance in each entry. A list of abbreviations/acronyms related to money, banking and finance is given on pages xi to xiv of the dictionary.
5. The dictionary also contains some essay type entries pertaining to important terms/institutions. These are meant to provide the reader an integrated view of the entry concerned as, for example, **Reserve Bank of India** which is the apex financial institution in the country.

Though adequate care has been taken to include in the dictionary as many terms and concepts as possible, a few omissions are likely in this kind of endeavour. I will feel obliged to be informed of such omissions that could find place in the next edition. Similarly, suggestions are welcome to improve the completeness and accuracy of the terms explained in the dictionary.

Several sources, such as books, articles, websites, have been referred to compile this work. I would like to thank all the published and other sources from which definitions have been gathered. Thanks are also due to the members of the research team of New Century Publications who actively contributed with their expertise during the preparation of the dictionary.

Kozhencherry
May 2014

Benson Kunjukunju

---

*q.v. = quod vide (Latin) = which may be referred to

Abbreviations/Acronyms Related to Money, Banking and Finance

ACLF	Additional Collateralised Lending Facility
ACU	Asian Clearing Union
ADB	Asian Development Bank
ADR	Assets Development Reserve
ADRs	American Depository Receipts
Ads	Authorised Dealers
AIDBs	All India Development Banks
AIFIs	All India Financial Institutions
ALM	Asset Liability Management
AML	Anti-Money Laundering
ATMs	Automated Teller Machines
BCBS	Basel Committee for Banking Supervision
BCSBI	Banking Codes and Standards Board of India
BFS	Board for Financial Supervision
BIFR	Board for Industrial and Financial Reconstruction
BIS	Bank for International Settlements
BPSS	Board for Payment and Settlement Systems
CAAP	Capital Adequacy Assessment Process
CAC	Capital Account Convertibility
CAMELS	Capital Adequacy, Asset Quality, Management, Earnings, Liquidity and Systems Control
CAR	Capital to Assets Ratio
CBLO	Collateralised Borrowing and Lending Obligations
CCIL	Clearing Corporation of India Ltd.
CDOs	Collateralised Debt Obligations
CDR	Corporate Debt Restructuring
CDR	Credit-Deposit Ratio
CDs	Certificates of Deposit
CIBIL	Credit Information Bureau of India Ltd.
CP	Commercial Paper
CPSS	Committee on Payment and Settlement Systems
CPSUs	Central Public Sector Undertakings

CR	Contingency Reserve
CRAR	Capital to Risk-Weighted Assets Ratio
CRISIL	Credit Rating Information Services of India Ltd.
CRR	Cash Reserve Ratio
DFIs	Development Finance Institutions
DIC	Deposit Insurance Corporation
DICGC	Deposit Insurance and Credit Guarantee Corporation
DPs	Depository Participants
DRI	Differential Rate of Interest
DRT	Debt Recovery Tribunals
DSR	Debt Service Ratio
ECBs	External Commercial Borrowings
E-Commerce	Electronic Commerce
ECR	Export Credit Refinance
ECS	Electronic Clearing Service
EFF	Extended Fund Facility
EFT	Electronic Funds Transfer
EMEs	Emerging Market Economies
E-Money	Electronic Money
EMU	European Monetary Union
EU	European Union
EXIM Bank	Export Import Bank of India
FCCBs	Foreign Currency Convertible Bonds
FCNR(A)	Foreign Currency Non-Resident (Accounts)
FCNR(B)	Foreign Currency Non-Resident Accounts (Banks)
FDI	Foreign Direct Investment
FEMA	Foreign Exchange Management Act
FERA	Foreign Exchange Regulation Act
FIIs	Foreign Institutional Investors
GIC	General Insurance Corporation of India
HDFC	Housing Development Finance Corporation Ltd.
IBA	Indian Banks' Association
IBRD	International Bank for Reconstruction and Development

ICICI	Industrial Credit and Investment Corporation of India
IDBI	Industrial Development Bank of India
IDFC	Infrastructure Development Finance Company
IFC	International Finance Corporation
IFCI	Industrial Finance Corporation of India Ltd.
IRDA	Insurance Regulatory and Development Authority
IRS	Interest Rate Swaps
ISDA	International Swap and Derivatives Association
IT	Information Technology
ITES	Information Technology Enabled Services
JLG	Joint Liability Group
KCC	Kisan Credit Card
LAF	Liquidity Adjustment Facility
LAN	Local Area Network
LERMS	Liberalised Exchange Rate Management System
LIBOR	London Inter-Bank Offered Rate
LIC	Life Insurance Corporation of India
MAT	Minimum Alternative Tax
MFs	Mutual Funds
MNCs	Multinational Companies
MoU	Memorandum of Understanding
NABARD	National Bank for Agriculture and Rural Development
NBFCs	Non-Banking Financial Companies
NEFT	National Electronic Funds Transfer
NHB	National Housing Bank
NLR	Net Liquidity Ratio
NPAs	Non-Performing Assets
NSE	National Stock Exchange
OMO	Open-Market Operations
OTC	Over the Counter
PLR	Prime Lending Rate
PPP	Purchasing Power Parity

PSBs	Public Sector Banks
PSU	Public Sector Undertaking
RBI	Reserve Bank of India
RBIA	Risk-Based Internal Audit
RBS	Risk-Based Supervision
REPO	Repurchase Agreement
RRBs	Regional Rural Banks
SBI	State Bank of India
SCBs	Scheduled Commercial Banks
SDRs	Special Drawing Rights
SEBI	Securities and Exchange Board of India
SEZ	Special Economic Zone
SHG	Self-help Group
SIDBI	Small Industries Development Bank of India
SLR	Statutory Liquidity Ratio
SSIs	Small Scale Industries
TBs	Treasury Bills
UCBs	Urban Cooperative Banks
UTI	Unit Trust of India
VAT	Value Added Tax
WMA	Ways and Means Advances
WTO	World Trade Organization

List of Entries

The Dictionary
A-Z

Aa

Absorptive Capacity: It is a hypothesis maintaining that as the rate of investment in an economy increases, the productivity of new investment declines. Because of its implications as a constraint of growth, the term has relevance in development economics. In his *General Theory of Employment, Interest and Money* (1936), British economist J.M. Keynes (1883-1946) used the term *marginal efficiency of capital* for productivity of new investment and believed that it declines with the rate of new investment. The explanation offered is that as investment increases, less and less suitable equipment is employed in the production process.

Accelerated Depreciation: It is a method under which entrepreneurs are allowed—during the first year or the first few years after acquiring business assets—to have depreciation allowances on a basis which exceeds the actual depreciation. This system provides incentive for capital investment by reducing the tax payable in the early years of the life of the assets concerned.

Acceptance Credit: It is a short-term financing facility under which the borrower draws bills of exchange on a bank which accepts them and discounts them in the market to provide cash for the borrower.

Account History: The payment history of an account over a specific period of time, including the number of times the account was past due or over limit.

Account Holder: Any and all persons designated and authorized to transact business on behalf of an account. Each account holder's signature needs to be on file with the bank. The signature authorizes that person to conduct business on behalf of the account.

Accrual Basis Accounting: There are two main methods of accounting: accrual basis accounting and Cash Basis Accounting (q.v.). Under the accrual method (also called mercantile method), income tax is calculated with reference to income earned and sales made during the taxable period. Net profit/loss of a business is calculated by taking into account income and expenditure of a particular accounting year, irrespective of the fact whether such income is received or not, and expenditure is actually incurred or not during the accounting period. Thus, income of a business accrued during the previous year is taxable whether it is received during the previous year or in a year following the previous year. Similarly, expenditure relating to previous year is deductible even if it is not incurred in the previous year.

Accrued Income: It is the income earned during a particular accounting period but not actually received during that period. Examples include interest credited (instead of paid), and appreciation in the value of assets (capital gains) which continue to be held.

Accumulated Depreciation: It is the total depreciation expense accrued from the date of purchase of an asset to the present.

Acquiring Bank: In a merger, it is the bank that absorbs the bank acquired.

Actuary: Actuary is a person trained in the calculation of risk and premiums for assurance purposes. The primary function of an actuary is to monitor the financial position of the company on a sustained basis. He or she is supposed to continuously investigate the matters such as adequacy of reserves to meet the liabilities, the level to which solvency margin requirements are met, the investment policy of the company, the new products being introduced and their price etc. Based upon these investigations, the actuary is supposed to keep informed the management and directors of the company and also to the regulator on a continuous basis. In some of the countries, the actuary may even directly report to the regulator. The management of the company is supposed to take corrective measures as recommended by the actuary, if so required.

***Ad Valorem* Duty:** A custom duty, an excise levy or a sales tax may be imposed either on *ad valorem* (according to value) basis or on specific basis. An *ad valorem* duty is imposed as a fixed percentage of the price of the product taxed. This form of duty is preferred when a commodity has many classifications and sub-classifications, e.g. textiles. An *ad valorem* duty is responsive to price changes and thus ensures an undiminished proportion of taxes in national income. The main problem in applying *ad valorem* rate is the determination of the tax base, i.e. valuation of production.

An *ad valorem* duty may be a simple one, a duty collected as a fixed proportion of the price irrespective of the price range. As a variant of this, the commodity in question may be completely exempted till the price reaches a pre-determined maximum level. When different duty rates apply to different price brackets of a commodity, it becomes a graduated or bracketed *ad valorem* duty. So long as the price remains within a single bracket, the rate of the duty remains the same. Generally, commodities in higher price brackets bear a higher duty rate and vice versa. See also Specific Duty.

Adjustable-rate Mortgages: Also known as variable-rate mortgages, the initial interest rate is usually below that of conventional fixed-rate loans. The interest rate may change over the life of the loan as market conditions change. There is typically a maximum (or ceiling) and a minimum (or floor) defined in the loan agreement. If interest rates rise, so does the loan payment. If interest rates fall, the loan payment may fall as well.

ADR: See American Depository Receipt, *6*.

Advance Ruling: It is issued by the tax administration of a country regarding the manner in which a particular future activity/transaction would be treated for tax purposes. Entrepreneurs planning certain business initiatives may approach tax authorities to find out tax implications of their intended activity. A request for advance ruling is generally in the form of an application containing all relevant facts and surrounding circumstances. A modest fee may also be charged for the purpose. Countries where advance ruling can be obtained include United States, Sweden, and the Netherlands. By binding the tax administration, an advance ruling creates certainty in the mind of the entrepreneur about the tax consequences of his activity.

Advance Tax Payment: It is a system under which assessees are required to pay tax in advance on incomes which they expect to earn during the current financial year. Advance tax, payable in instalments during the financial year itself, is adjusted against the tax liability determined after proper assessment. Under Section 208 of the Indian Income Tax Act, 1961, it is obligatory to pay advance tax in every case where the advance tax payable is ₹ 10,000 or more. See also Withholding Tax.

All Risks Coverage: It is a type of marine insurance which provides the broadest kind of standard coverage, but excludes damage caused by war, strikes, and riots.

American Depository Receipt (ADR): A certificate issued in US in lieu of a foreign security. The original securities are lodged in bank/custodian abroad, and the ADRs are traded in the US for all intents and purposes as if they were a domestic stock. An ADR dividend is paid in US dollars, so it provides a way for American investors to buy foreign securities without having to go abroad, and without having to switch in and out of foreign currencies.

Amortization: In finance, it means the gradual repayment of a debt by means of a sinking fund. Thus, amortisation of debt means gradual reduction of a debt through periodic payments. In another context amortisation of an asset (machinery) refers to depreciation in its value over time.

Annuity: It is a fixed sum of money paid to an annuitant yearly, usually for the remaining part of his life. It is a form of pension which provides a regular annual income. An annuity may be purchased by making a lump sum cash payment.

Anti-trust Policy: It prohibits monopoly, restraints of trade and other practices to inhibit competition. Although many countries have adopted anti-trust legislations, US was the first to do so when the Federal law, the Sherman Anti-trust Act, 1890 outlawed monopolies and restraints of trade. This Act was revised and strengthened by another Federal statute, namely Clayton Anti-trust Act enacted in 1914. In India, anti-trust policy is pursued through the Monopolies and Restrictive Trade Practices Act, 1968.

Appreciation of Currency: It refers to gradual increase in the external value of a currency in a free and fluctuating exchange market over several days/weeks. The increase is generally due to favourable supply and demand factors and without any specific or deliberate attempt made by monetary authorities to do so.

Arbitrage: It is a term used in the context of international short-term capital flows. It refers to profiting by buying some financial asset/currency at a lower price and selling at a higher price in two different markets when both prices are known to the trader. So, there is no risk involved in it. For example, if dollar is cheaper in Kuwait than in Singapore, arbitrageurs will buy it in Kuwait and sell in Singapore. This will continue till the two rates are equal. If the exchange rates in various centres (more than two) are made mutually consistent, it is called *triangular arbitrage.*

Asian Development Bank (ADB): This multilateral development finance institution is engaged in promoting economic and social progress of its developing member countries in the Asian and

Pacific region. Its headquarters are in Manila, Philippines. The Bank began its operations in December 1966. It is owned by the governments of 40 countries from the region and 16 countries from outside the region.

Over the years, ADB has been a catalyst in promoting the development of the most populous region in the world. It provides technical assistance for the preparation and execution of development projects and programmes. It promotes investment of public and private capital for development purposes. ADB gives special attention to the needs of the smaller and less developed countries. It gives priority to regional, sub-regional, and national projects and programmes which contribute to the harmonious economic growth of the region as a whole and which promote regional co-operation.

Asset: Ownership of any physical property or right that has money value is called asset. Land, buildings, machinery and other forms of physical property are called *tangible assets*. Goodwill, patents, trademarks, copyrights and other non-material benefits are called *intangible assets*. Similarly, cash in hand, marketable securities, inventories and other assets which can be readily converted into money are called *current assets* while plant, equipment and time deposits are *fixed assets* because they are not readily convertible into money.

Asset Securitisation: Securitisation is a process through which illiquid assets are transformed into a more liquid form of assets and distributed to a broad range of investors through capital markets. The lending institution's assets are removed from its balance sheet and are instead funded by investors through a negotiable financial instrument. The security is backed by the expected cash flows from the assets. Securitisation as a technique gained popularity in the advanced countries in the 1970s. Favourable tax treatment, legislative enactments, establishment of Government-backed institutions that extend guarantees, and a pragmatic regulatory environment appear to have contributed to the successful development of this market.

Securitisation involves pooling similar assets together in a separate legal entity or special purpose vehicle (SPV) and redirecting the cash flows from the asset pool to the new securities issued by the SPV. The SPV is a device to ensure that the underlying assets are insulated from the risks of default by the originator of the assets. In general, there are two main advantages of securitisation. First, it can turn ordinary illiquid assets into reasonably liquid instruments. Second, it can create instruments of high credit quality out of debt of low credit quality.

Securitisation is designed to offer a number of advantages to the seller, investor and the debt market. For the seller or originator, securitisation mainly results in receivables being replaced by cash, thereby improving the liquidity position. It removes the assets from the balance sheet of the originator, thus, freeing capital for other uses, and enabling restructuring of the balance sheet by reducing large exposures or sectoral concentration. It facilitates better asset liability management (ALM) by reducing market risks resulting from interest rate mismatches. The process also enables the issuer to recycle assets more frequently and thereby improves earnings. For investors, securitisation essentially provides an avenue for relatively lower risk investment. Credit enhancement provides an opportunity to investors to acquire good quality assets and to diversify their portfolios. From the point of view of the financial system as a whole, securitisation increases the number of debt instruments in the market, and provides additional liquidity in the market. It also facilitates unbundling, better allocation and management of project risks. It widens the market by attracting new players due to availability of superior quality assets.

Securitisation, however, if not carried out prudently can leave risks with the originating bank without allocating capital to back them. The main risk for a bank arises if a true sale has not been achieved and the selling bank is forced to recognise some or all of the losses if the assets subsequently cease to perform. Also, funding risks and constraints on liquidity may arise if assets designed to be securitised have been originated, but because of disturbances in the market, the securities cannot be placed. There is also a view that there is at least a potential conflict of interest if bank originates, sells, services and underwrites the same issue of securities.

Assets of a Bank: See Commercial Bank, *37*.

ATM: See Automated Teller Machine, *10*.

Audit: An investigation of an assessee's accounts by an independent certified accountancy firm or tax department. It is common for tax authorities to demand that accounts rendered by an assessee in connection with declaration of his income or profits are correct. Investigation of an assessee's books and accounts may also be done by tax authorities as a routine operation or where evasion is suspected. The audit requirement is generally embodied in the tax law, particularly for large business organisations.

Automated Clearing House (ACH): A computerized facility used by member depository institutions to electronically combine, sort, and distribute inter-bank credits and debits. ACHs process electronic transfers of government securities and provide customer services, such as direct deposit of customers' salaries and government benefit payments (i.e. social security, welfare entitlements etc.), and pre-authorized transfers.

Automated Teller Machine (ATM): A machine, activated by a magnetically encoded card or other medium that can process a variety of banking transactions. These include accepting deposits and loan payments, providing withdrawals, and transferring funds between accounts.

Automatic Bill Payment: A cheque less system for paying recurring bills with one authorization statement to a financial institution. For example, the customer would only have to provide one authorization form/letter/document to pay the cable bill each month. The necessary debits and credits are made through an automated clearing house.

Available Balance: It is the balance of an account less any hold, uncollected funds, and restrictions against the account.

Available Credit: It is the difference between the credit limit assigned to a cardholder account and the present balance of the account.

Bb

Bad Debt: It is a loan which is not likely to be repaid due to borrower's insolvency or dishonesty.

Balance of International Indebtedness: It is a statement of the net claims of the residents of a country against the residents of the rest of the world. Also known as *international investment position* or b*alance sheet for the foreign sector,* it is derived from all debits and credits in the capital account of a country's balance of payments measured at the prevailing exchange rate. From this, one can know a country's net credit or net debit position. It also reflects the liquidity position of a country, i.e. how does the maturity structure of assets compare with the maturity structure of liabilities. If assets are mainly long-term and liabilities short-term, there can be a liquidity problem for the country.

Balance of Payments: The balance of payments is a statistical summary of international transactions. These transactions are defined as the transfer of ownership of something that has an economic value measurable in monetary terms from residents of one country to residents of another. The transfer may involve: (a) goods, which consist of tangible and visible commodities or products; (b) services, which consist of intangible economic outputs, which usually must be produced, transferred, and consumed at the same time and in the same place; (c) income on investments; and (d) financial claims on, and liabilities to, the rest of the world, including changes in a country's reserve assets held by the central monetary authorities.

Generally, a transaction is the exchange of one asset for another or one asset for several assets, but it may also involve a gift, which is the provision by one party of something of economic value to another party without something of economic value being received in return. International transactions are recorded in the balance of payments on the basis of the double-entry principle used in business accounting, in which each transaction gives rise to two offsetting entries of equal value so that, in principle, the resulting credit and debit entries always balance. Transactions are generally valued at market prices and are, to the extent possible, recorded when a change of ownership occurs. Transactions in goods, services, income, and unilateral transfers constitute the current account, and transactions in financial assets and liabilities constitute the capital account.

The International Monetary Fund, which strives for international comparability, defines the balance of payments as "a statistical statement for a given period showing (a) transactions in goods, services, and income between an economy and the rest of the world, (b) changes of ownership and other changes in that economy's monetary gold, special drawing rights (SDRs), and claims on and liabilities to the rest of the world and (c) unrequited transfers and counterpart entries that are needed to balance, in the accounting sense, any entries for the foregoing transactions and changes which are not mutually offsetting".

Balance of Trade: It is the difference between merchandise exports and imports of a country. It is the most important category in balance of payments. Since data on exports and imports are available sooner than on other items, it shows the trends of balance of payments quite early.

Balance Sheet of a Commercial Bank: See Commercial Bank, *37*.

Balance Transfer: The process of moving an outstanding balance from one credit card to another. This is usually done to obtain a lower interest rate on the outstanding balance. Transfers are sometimes subjected to a balance transfer fee.

Bancassurance: The phenomenon whereby a financial institution combines the selling of banking products and insurance products through the same distribution channel. Bancassurance rests on the premise that it is easy to cross-sell banking and insurance services because customers feel confident buying insurance from the same institution where they keep their savings.

Bank Custodian: A bank custodian is responsible for maintaining the safety of clients' assets held at one of the custodian's premises, a sub-custodian facility or an outside depository.

Bank Examination: Examination of a bank's assets, income, and expenses, as well as operations by supervisory authorities, to ensure that the bank is solvent and is operating in conformity with banking laws and sound banking principles.

Bank for International Settlements (BIS): This bank was set up at the Hague Conference in January 1930 to help in the collection of German reparation payments. It consisted of Belgium, France, Germany, Italy, Japan, UK and US. Later on it acted as a clearing office for European Payments Union (EPU), i.e. to keep records of inter-country debit/credit entries of each EPU member-country with non-EPU countries. The BIS has always been a central banking institution which is unique at the international level. It is owned and controlled by central banks and it provides a number of highly-specialised services to central banks and through them to the international financial system more generally. At present, BIS is actively deepening its relationships with central banks outside its traditional focus in the industrialised world. The BIS commenced its activities in Basel on May 17, 1930 and is thus the world's oldest international financial organisation. Presently, Basel has become the traditional international meeting place for many central bank governors and other officials.

Bank Guarantee: An assurance, obtained from a bank by a foreign purchaser that the bank will pay an exporter up to a given amount for goods shipped if the foreign purchaser defaults.

Bank Rate: See Reserve Bank of India, *191*.

Bank Release: Negotiable time draft drawn on and accepted by a bank which adds its credit to that of an importer of merchandise.

Bank Statement: Periodically the bank provides a statement of a customer's deposit account. It shows all deposits made, all cheques paid, and other debits posted during the period (usually one month), as well as the current balance.

Banker's Acceptance: A banker's acceptance is a draft drawn on and accepted by a bank. Depending on the bank's creditworthiness, the acceptance becomes a financial instrument which can be discounted.

Banking Codes and Standards Board of India (BCSBI): The RBI's Committee on Procedures and Performance Audit of Public Services (Chairman: S.S. Tarapore), 2003 had recommended that BCSBI be set up as an independent organisation but strongly supported and fully funded by the RBI. Accordingly, in the Annual Policy Statement of the RBI for 2005-06, it was proposed to set up an independent Banking Codes and Standards Board of India on the lines of the Banking Code of the British Bankers' Association of the UK in order to ensure that comprehensive code of conduct for fair treatment of customers is evolved and adhered to.

Banking Ombudsman Scheme: It was introduced effective January 1, 2006 with the object of enabling resolution of complaints relating to certain services rendered by banks and to facilitate the satisfaction or settlement of such complaints. The scheme is primarily meant for redressal of grievances against deficiency in banking services, concerning loans and advances and other specified matters.

Bankrupt: A bankrupt person, firm, or company has insufficient assets to cover its debts. The debtor seeks relief through a court proceeding to work out a payment schedule or erase debts. In some cases, the debtor must surrender control of all assets to a court-appointed trustee.

Bankruptcy: It means the legal proceedings by which the affairs of a bankrupt person are turned over to a trustee or receiver for administration under the bankruptcy laws. There are two types of bankruptcy: (a) involuntary bankruptcy—one or more creditors of an insolvent debtor file a petition having the debtor declared bankrupt and (b) voluntary bankruptcy—the debtor files a petition claiming inability to meet financial obligations and willingness to be declared bankrupt.

Base Currency: It is the currency against which the exchange rate of another currency is determined. For example, if rupee is quoted at ₹ 61 = 1 US$, then dollar is the base currency. Rupee is the quoted currency.

Basel I Norms: Internationally, there were no explicit capital adequacy standards before the introduction of Basel I norms in 1988. The most common approach was to lay down minimum capital requirements for banks in the respective banking legislations and determine the relative strength of capital position of a bank by ratios such as debt-equity ratio, or its other variants for measuring the level of leverage.

In the autumn of 1974, the Bank of England began to conceptualise the formation of a G-10 group of bank supervisors leading to the formation of the Standing Committee on Banking Regulation and Supervisory Practices, or the Basel Committee, in December 1974. The initial mandate of the Committee was for sharing of and application of each others knowledge, rather than any comprehensive attempt to harmonise cross-country supervision. Nevertheless, it led to an unimaginable degree of regulatory harmonisation later.

In December 1987 International Convergence of Capital Measures and Capital Standards, i.e. Basel Accord (now Basel I) was achieved. In July 1988, the Basel I Capital Accord was created.

The major achievement of the Basel Capital Accord, 1988, was the introduction of discipline through imposition of risk-based capital standards both as measure of the strength of banks and as a trigger device for intervention by supervisors under the scheme of prompt corrective action (PCA).

Over the years, however, several deficiencies of the design of the Basel I framework surfaced. The Basel I capital adequacy norms were criticised for the simple *one-size-fits-all* approach that did not adequately differentiate between assets that have different risk levels. Despite the amendment to the original framework in 1996, the simple risk weighting approach of Basel I did not keep pace with more advanced risk measurement approaches at large banking organisations. By the late 1990s, some large banking organisations, especially in advanced countries, had begun developing economic capital models, which used quantitative methods to estimate the amount of capital required to support various elements of risks of an organization.

The Basel Committee itself recognised the deficiencies in the Basel I framework. The rapid rate of innovation in financial markets and the growing complexity of financial transactions reduced the relevance of Basel I as a risk managing framework, especially for large and complex banking organisations. Various shortcomings also distorted the behaviour of banks and made it much more complicated to monitor them.

Given the financial innovations and growing complexity of financial transactions and also with a view to addressing the shortcomings of Basel I, the Basel Committee on Banking Supervision (BCBS) released the New Capital Adequacy Framework for International Convergence of Capital Measurement and Capital Standards (Basel II) on June 26, 2004 to replace the 1988 Capital Accord by year-end 2007. Basel II norms (q.v.) aim at aligning minimum capital requirements to underlying risk profiles of banks. The framework is also designed to create incentives for better risk measurement and management.

Basel II Norms: While the Basel I norms (q.v.) were confined to the minimum capital requirements for banks, the Basel II accord expands this approach to include two additional areas, *viz.* the supervisory review process and increased disclosure requirements for banks. In terms of Basel II, the stability of the banking system rests on the following three pillars, which are designed to reinforce each other:

Pillar 1: Minimum Capital Requirements—a largely new, risk-adequate calculation of capital requirements which (for the first time) explicitly includes operational risk in addition to market and credit risk.

Pillar 2: Supervisory Review Process (SRP)—the establishment of suitable risk management systems in banks and their review by the supervisory authority.

Pillar 3: Market Discipline—increased transparency due to expanded disclosure requirements for banks.

The central focus of this framework as in Basel I, continues to be credit risk. In the revised framework, the minimum regulatory capital requirements take into account not just credit risk and market risk, but also operational risk. The measures for credit risk are more complex, for market risk they are the same, while those for operational risk are new. Besides, Basel II includes certain Pillar 2 risks such as credit concentration risks and liquidity risks.

Apart from an increase in the number of risks, banks are required to achieve a more comprehensive risk management framework. While Basel I required lenders to calculate a minimum level of capital based on a single risk weight for each of the limited number of asset classes, the capital requirements are more risk sensitive under Basel II. The credit risk weights are related directly to the credit rating of each counterparty instead of the counterparty category.

Basel II capital adequacy rules are based on a *menu* approach that allows differences in approaches in relationship to the nature of banks and the nature of markets in which they operate. The minimum requirements for the advanced approaches are technically more demanding and require extensive databases and more sophisticated risk management techniques. Basel II prescriptions have ushered in a transition from capital adequacy to capital efficiency which implies that banks adopt a more dynamic use of capital, in which capital will flow quickly to its most efficient uses. Unlike Basel I, Basel II is quite complex as it offers choices, some of which involve application of quantitative techniques.

The revised framework is designed to provide options to banks and banking systems for determining the capital requirements for credit risk, market risk and operational risk. It enables banks/supervisors to select approaches that are most appropriate for their operations and financial markets. The revised framework is expected to promote adoption of stronger risk management practices in banks. Under Basel II, capital requirements of banks will be more closely aligned with the underlying risks in the balance sheets of banks.

Operational Risk: One of the important features of the revised framework is the emphasis on operational risk. Operational risk is defined as the risk of loss resulting from inadequate or failed internal processes, people and systems or from external events. This definition includes legal risk, but excludes strategic and reputational risks. Operational risk differs from other banking risks in that it is typically not directly taken in return for an expected reward but is implicit in the ordinary course of corporate activity and has the potential to affect the risk management process. The Basel Committee identified the following seven types of operational risk events that have the potential to result in substantial losses.

1. Internal fraud.
2. External fraud.
3. Employment practices and workplace safety.
4. Clients, products and business practices.
5. Damage to physical assets.
6. Business disruption and system failures.
7. Execution, delivery and process management.

The potential losses, in turn, vary according to the business line within the bank in which the event occurs.

Management of specific operational risks is not new. It has always been important for banks to try to prevent fraud, maintain the integrity of internal controls, reduce errors in transaction processing and so on. However, what is relatively new is the thrust on operational risk management as a comprehensive practice comparable to the management of credit risk and market risk. To manage operational risk, banks are gradually gearing to develop risk assessment techniques that are appropriate to the size and complexities of portfolios, their resources and data availability.

Implementation of Basel Norms in India: India has been adopting international best practices in the area of regulation and supervision with a view to strengthening the banking sector. Following the Basel Accord of 1988, the capital to risk-weighted assets ratio (CRAR)—which took into account the element of risk involved in both balance sheet as well as off-balance sheet business—emerged as a well-recognised and universally accepted measure of soundness of the banking system. Accordingly, as a part of banking sector reforms, India adopted the Basel norms in a phased manner. In fact, India went a step further and stipulated CRAR at 9 percent as against the international norm of 8 percent. Furthermore, India also prescribed the capital charge for market risk in June 2004, broadly in line with the 1996 amendment to Basel norms.

In order to ensuring migration to Basel II in a non-disruptive manner, given the complexities involved, a consultative approach was followed. The RBI released draft guidelines for implementation of Basel II in India on February 15, 2005. In terms of the draft guidelines, banks were required to adopt standardised approach for credit risk and basic indicator approach for operational risk. The standardised duration method would continue to be applied to arrive at the capital charge for market risk. Banks would need the RBI's approval for migration to advanced approaches of risk measurement.

With a view to ensuring smooth transition to the revised framework and providing opportunity to banks to streamline their systems and strategies, banks were required to commence a parallel run of the revised framework with effect from April 1, 2006. All scheduled commercial banks (except regional rural banks) were required to implement the revised capital adequacy framework with effect from March 31, 2007. However, Basel II framework in India became fully operational from end-March 2009.

Several measures were undertaken by the RBI to prepare the banking system to make a smooth migration to Basle II. Following the amendment to the Banking Companies (Acquisition and Transfer of Undertakings) Act in 1994, several public sector banks (PSBs) have raised capital both in India and abroad through Global Depository Receipts (GDRs). Several PSBs have also raised subordinated debt through the private placement. Concurrently, a series of regulatory initiatives were taken by the RBI relevant for Basel II.

First, concerted efforts were made to ensure that the banks had suitable risk management framework oriented towards their requirements, dictated by the size and complexity of business, risk philosophy, market perceptions and the expected level of capital. Second, Risk Based Supervision (RBS) was introduced in 23 banks on a pilot basis. Third, the RBI encouraged the banks to formalise their Internal Capital Adequacy Assessment Programme (ICAAP) in alignment with their business plans and performance budgeting system. Fourth, there has been a marked improvement in the area of disclosures, so as to have greater transparency in the financial position and risk profile of banks. Similarly, capacity building for ensuring the regulator's ability for identifying and permitting eligible banks to adopt Internal Ratings Based/Advanced Measurement approaches was given due priority.

The implementation of Basel II requires closer cooperation, information sharing and coordination of policies among sectoral supervisors, especially in the context of financial conglomerates.

Bear Market: A market in which, in a time of falling prices, shareholders may rush to sell their stock shares, adding to the downward momentum.

Beneficiary: A person who is entitled to receive the benefits or proceeds of a will, trust, insurance policy, retirement plan, annuity, or other contract.

Bilateral Aid: See Foreign Aid, *95*.

Bill of Exchange: It is a written binding by the signer or signers to pay a certain sum at a future day or on demand, with or without interest, as may be stated in the document. The bill of exchange looks something like a cheque which is drawn on an overseas buyer, or even on a third party, as designated in the export contact, for the sum agreed as settlement. An exporter can send a bill of exchange for the value of goods for export through the banking system for payment by an overseas buyer on presentation. The bill is called a sight draft if it is made out payable at sight, i.e. *on demand.* If it is payable *at a fixed or determinable future time* it is called a term draft, because the buyer is receiving a period of credit, known as the tenor of the bill.

Bill of Lading (B/L): B/L is common when goods are shipped by sea or where goods are packed in a container. B/L serves three main purposes: (a) it acts as evidence that there is a contract between either the exporter or importer and a chipping company to transport the goods by sea, (b) it is a receipt for goods shipped and provides certain details as to their condition when placed on board, and (c) it is also a document of title, which means that the company named in the B/L has the right to possess the goods. A transfer of title in the B/L will transfer the ownership. This element of the B/L is vital to the payment arrangements for the goods. Bills of lading are made out in sets of two or three originals, any one of them gives title to the goods.

Ocean Bill of Lading: A receipt for the cargo and a contract for transportation between a shipper and the ocean carrier. It may also be used as an instrument of ownership which can be bought, sold, or traded while the goods are in transit. To be used in this manner, it must be a negotiable Order Bill of Lading.

Clean Bill of Lading: It is issued when the shipment is received in good order. If damaged or a shortage is noted, a clean bill of lading will not be issued.

On Board Bill of Lading: It certifies that the cargo has been placed aboard the named vessel and is signed by the master of the vessel or his representative. On letter of credit transactions, an On Board B/L is usually necessary for the shipper to obtain payment from the bank.

Inland Bill of Lading: It is a waybill on rail or the pro forma bill of lading in trucking that is used to document the transportation of the goods between the port and the point of origin or destination. It should contain information such as marks, numbers, steamship line, and similar information to match with a dock receipt.

Through Bill of Lading: A single bill of lading covering receipt of the cargo at the point of origin for delivery to the ultimate consignee, using two or more modes of transportation.

Billing Cycle: The time interval between the dates on which regular periodic statements are issued.

Billing Error: A charge that appears on a periodic statement associated with an extension of credit (e.g. credit card). A billing error can be caused by a creditor's failure to credit a payment or other credit to an account as well as accounting and clerical errors.

Black Money: The term black money stands for money earned by illegal means and kept secretly and unaccounted for. It is widely used for smuggling activities, hoarding of scarce commodities (for purposes of speculation, profiteering and black marketing), bribing government officials, financing political activities, and ostentatious living. Secret business deals through black money in turn lead to tax evasion and a vicious circle is created in which one evil thrives on the other.

Blue Chip: The term refers to the shares of a large reputed company whose earnings and dividend records have been stable or growing over the years. Blue chip shares are generally priced high in relation to a company's earnings due to its good reputation.

Board for Financial Supervision (BFS): BFS was constituted by the RBI in November 1994 to exercise *undivided attention to supervision*. The BFS provides direction on a continuing basis on supervisory policies including governance issues and supervisory practices. It also provides direction on supervisory actions in specific cases. The BFS ensures an integrated approach to supervision of commercial banks, financial institutions, non-banking financial companies, urban co-operatives banks and primary dealers.

Bombay Stock Exchange (BSE): BSE is a stock exchange located on Dalal Street, Mumbai. It was the 11th largest stock exchange in the world by market capitalisation as on December 31, 2012. Established in 1875, BSE Ltd. (formerly known as Bombay Stock Exchange Ltd.), is India's second oldest stock exchange (Oldest being the Calcutta Stock Exchange located at Lyons Range, Kolkata) and one of India's leading exchange groups.

In August 31, 1957, the BSE became the first stock exchange to be recognized by the Indian Government under the Securities Contracts Regulation Act. In 1980 the exchange moved to the Phiroze Jeejeebhoy Towers at Dalal Street, Fort area. In 1986 it developed the BSE SENSEX index, giving the BSE a means to measure overall performance of the exchange. In 2000 the BSE used this index to open its derivatives market, trading SENSEX futures contracts. The development of SENSEX options along with equity derivatives followed in 2001 and 2002, expanding the BSE's trading platform.

BSE has facilitated the growth of the Indian corporate sector by providing it an efficient capital-raising platform. BSE is a corporatized and demutualised entity, with a broad chorholder-base which includes two leading global exchanges, Deutsche Bourse, Fuse and Singapore Exchange as strategic partners. BSE provides an efficient and transparent market for trading in equity, debt instruments, derivatives, mutual funds. It also has a platform for trading in equities of small-and-medium enterprises (SME). More than 5,000 companies are listed on BSE making it world's Number 1 exchange in terms of listed members. BSE is world's fifth most active exchange in terms of number of transactions handled through its electronic trading system. It is also one of the world's leading exchanges (5th largest in December 2013) for Index options trading (Source: World Federation of Exchanges).

BSE also provides a host of other services to capital market participants including risk management, clearing, settlement, market data services and education. It has a global reach with customers around the world and a nation-wide presence. BSE systems and processes are designed to safeguard market integrity, drive the growth of the Indian capital market and stimulate innovation and competition across all market segments. BSE is the first exchange in India and second in the world to obtain an ISO 9001:2000 certification. It is also the first exchange in the country and second in the world to receive Information Security Management System Standard BS 7799-2-2002 certification for its On-Line Trading System (BOLT).

It operates one of the most respected capital market educational institutes in the country (the BSE Institute Ltd.). BSE also provides depository services through its Central Depository Services Ltd. (CDSL) arm.

BSE's popular equity index—the S&P BSE SENSEX (formerly SENSEX)—is India's most widely tracked stock market benchmark index. It is traded internationally on the EUREX as well as leading exchanges of the BRCS nations (Brazil, Russia, China and South Africa). On February 19, 2013, BSE entered into Strategic Partnership with S&P DOW JONES INDICES and the

SENSEX was renamed as S&P BSE SENSEX.

Historically an open outcry floor trading exchange, the BSE switched to an electronic trading system in 1995. This automated, screen-based trading platform is called BSE On-line Trading (BOLT). The BSE has also introduced the world's first centralized exchange-based internet trading system, BSEWEBx.co.in to enable investors anywhere in the world to trade on the BSE platform.

Bond: A bond is a promise to pay a stated sum of money as interest each year and to repay the face value of bond at some future redemption date. Some bonds, called *perpetuities*, pay a fixed sum of interest each year forever but never repay the principal, i.e. they have no redemption date.

Bonded Goods: Imported goods stored in a bonded warehouse, usually after the owners of the goods have deposited a bond guaranteeing that the duty will be paid when and if the goods are withdrawn for domestic sale.

Bonded Warehouse: It is a warehouse licensed and bonded by the government to insure against loss of customs duty. Goods subject to customs duty may be stored there without paying duty. Such goods are said to be under bond. These storage facilities are operated under the lock and key of a country's customs authorities and the owners of these facilities are bonded to ensure that they will satisfy all customs duty obligations. The importer will have to pay the existing duty on the goods if they enter the domestic market. Sometimes, the stored goods are repacked or further processed there. However, if additional domestic materials are used they are exempt from duty, only the import portion is subject to customs duty.

Bonus Issue: It refers to shares issued by a company to existing shareholders not in respect of the subscription of new capital but as a capitalisation of reserves. The extra shares are issued free on a pro rata basis. They may not by themselves confer any benefits to shareholders. They bring the issued capital more into line with the real capital of the company which may have appreciated in value in money terms.

Book Value: It is the value at which equity or other capital asset or liability is recorded in the balance sheet of an entity. Book value can reflect one of the following valuation methods: (a) historical cost, (b) replacement cost, (c) an interim adjusted price, which is not the current market price, (d) fair market value, and (e) current market price.

Boom: It is a period of high output and high employment in an economy.

Break-even Point: It refers to that quantity of sales with which a firm neither makes profit nor incurs losses. Above this level, the firm starts earning profit, and below it, suffers losses. Breakeven point analysis is used to estimate profit/loss of a firm at various levels of output.

Bretton Woods Conference: This Conference of Allied Nations was held in July 1944 at Bretton Woods, New Hampshire, US. 44 countries participated in it and resolved to establish International Monetary Fund (IMF) (q.v.) and the International Bank for Reconstruction and Development (IBRD) (q.v.). An agreement was signed to provide a stable monetary environment to facilitate the economic reconstruction of the world after Second World War. The Conference itself was the outcome of lengthy trans-Atlantic negotiations. IMF was meant to symbolise a new international monetary system under which fixed exchange rate system (of nearly all principal currencies) was made the base.

Bridging Credit: It means borrowing ahead of receiving payment for a sale, or short-term credit to a customer pending his or her receipt of funds from another source.

BS7799: It is a standard to be followed by financial institutions (including banks) to ensure compliance to most of the information security requirements. It is comprehensive in its coverage of security issues, containing a significant number of control requirements. Hence, compliance with it is a major task for most organisations.

Budget: It is a financial plan listing expenditure and income expected during some given future period, usually one year. A budget may be prepared by an individual, a family, a company, or a government. Individuals and families expect income from salaries, interest-bearing securities, rent and gifts. They anticipate expenditure on food, clothing, housing, education, health care, entertainment etc. A company budget is usually based on expected output and sale proceeds, and anticipated expenses. A government budget is based on expected tax and non-tax revenues, and expenditure on defence, external affairs, educational institutions, hospitals, and a host of other administrative, developmental and maintenance activities. When income and expenditure are equal over some period of time, the budget is said to be balanced. In practice, even the most carefully planned budgets result in excess of income over expenditure (surplus budget) or excess of expenditure over income (deficit budget).

Budget Deficit: It is the amount each year by which government spending is greater than government income.

Budget Surplus: It is the amount each year by which government income exceeds government spending.

Buffer Stocks: The term refers to commodity stockpiles managed in such a way as to moderate price fluctuations. Goods may be sold from a stockpile when prices reach or approach pre-determined ceiling prices, and they may be purchased for the stockpile when prices reach or approach pre-determined floor levels. Rubber and cocoa are among the commodities considered most likely to benefit from buffer stocks, and international commodity agreements exist for both of these products.

Bull Market: A market in which there is a continuous rise in stock prices.

Business Cycles: Business cycles (also called trade cycles) are long-term patterns of fluctuations in economic activities in an economy. They are characteristic of a capitalistic economy.

Business Day: Any day on which offices of a bank are open to the public for carrying on substantially all of the bank's business.

Cc

Call Options: See Options, *169*.

Cancelled Cheque: A cheque that a bank has paid, charged to the account holder's account, and then endorsed. Once cancelled, a cheque is no longer negotiable.

Capital: It refers to all those man-made machines and appliances which are used for further production of goods and services rather than being consumed for their own sake.

Capital Account Convertibility (CAC): It allows freedom to make investment in foreign equity, extend loans to foreigners, buy real estate in foreign lands and vice versa. Broadly speaking, CAC allows anyone to move freely from local currency into foreign currency and back. See also Current Account Convertibility.

Capital Allowances: These are deductions from business income for depreciation of assets used in business. These are allowed because fixed assets (like plant and machinery) are gradually used up in the production process. If their wear and tear is not taken into account, the taxable income will be overstated. Annual capital allowances traditionally take the form of a fixed percentage of the cost of an asset.

Capital Expenditure: In the context of taxation of income, the distinction between capital expenditure and Revenue Expenditure (q.v.) is important because only revenue expenditure is allowed to be deducted while computing income. Capital expenditure is deductible to the extent of depreciation allowance permitted. Tax laws rarely define capital expenditure and revenue expenditure. Based on their natural meaning and judicial pronouncements, the two terms are understood in the following manner: (a) capital expenditure is incurred in acquiring fixed assets while revenue expenditure is made in the normal course of business, (b) capital expenditure produces benefits for several years while revenue expenditure is consumed within the same year, and (c) capital expenditure is of non-recurring nature while revenue expenditure is incurred again and again.

Capital Flight: It refers to erratic outflows of capital from one country to another in order to earn profit or avoid loss which may occur due to exchange rate variations. For example, fearing a fall in exchange rate, speculators may move foreign currency out of the country and bring it back after devaluation when it is worth more. A comprehensive exchange control regime can check capital flight.

Capital Formation: The excess of production over consumption in a year is called capital formation. It is also called accumulation. The entire production of a year is not consumed. Production is normally higher than consumption. The surplus of production over consumption in a year is defined as capital formation. Capital formation consists broadly of the following: (i) construction of new assets like buildings, roads and bridges, (ii) production of machinery and equipment, and (iii) increase in the stocks of raw materials, semi-finished goods and finished goods in a year.

Capital Gains: These gains arise from the sale of assets other than those held in the ordinary conduct of business. For example, gains from the sale of a house by the house owner are capital gains while gains from appreciation in the value of houses held by a real estate dealer are ordinary gains of business. The procedure to compute capital gains involves the following steps: (a) ascertain the full value of consideration received or accruing as a result of the transfer of the asset, (b) Deduct from the full value of consideration, (i) the cost of acquisition of the asset including cost of any improvements made to the asset, and (ii) expenditure incurred in connection with the transfer of such asset (brokerage, legal expenses etc.). See also Capital Loss.

Capital Gains Tax: It is a tax on the increase in capital value of an asset.

Capital Goods: Industrial products or other goods that are used in the creation of additional wealth, such as machine tools. Capital goods are sometimes called intermediate goods or producer goods, because they are used to produce other goods.

Capital Loss: It is a decrease in the value of an asset. In terms of the net accretion principle, capital losses are set off against capital gains and net capital losses are treated as a reduction in income (economic power) of an individual. See also Capital Gains.

Capital Market: Capital market is a market for long-term funds. The distinction between capital market and money market is not watertight. Broadly speaking, capital market focuses on financing of fixed investment (machinery and equipment) while money market provides working capital finance (raw material etc.). Capital market canalises household savings to the corporate sector and allocates funds to firms. In this process, it allows both firms and households to share risks associated with business. Moreover, capital market enables the valuation of firms on an almost continuous basis and plays an important role in the governance of the corporate sector.

An efficient capital market is an important constituent of a sound financial system. In India, efforts have been made in recent years to set up an effective regulatory framework covering major participants in the capital market. Similarly, the technology of trading and settlements in the stock exchanges has been upgraded. Internet-based trading in securities has been permitted. Foreign institutional investors (FIIs) and pension funds were allowed to enter the Indian stock market from 1993 onwards.

Capital Receipts: Those receipts of an organisation which create liability or reduce assets are called capital receipts. Thus, money obtained by way of loan, from the sale of fixed assets, issue of shares and debentures are capital receipts. They are generally of a non-recurring nature. Capital receipts are exempt from income tax unless they are expressly taxable whereas Revenue Receipts (q.v.) are taxable unless they are expressly exempt from tax.

Cash Basis Accounting: Under cash basis accounting, as against accrual basis accounting, a record is kept of actual receipts (cash incomings) and actual payments (cash outgoings) of a particular year. Thus, income collected during the previous year is taxable whether it relates to the previous year or a year preceding or following the previous year. Similarly, expenditure actually incurred during the previous year is deductible irrespective of the fact whether it relates to the previous year or some other year. Similarly, tax revenues of a government may be recorded either on cash basis (the time at which the tax payment was received by a government) or on an accrual basis (the time when payment became due without incurring any penalty). Under cash basis reporting, taxes due in one year but actually paid in the following year and taxes withheld by the employer in one year but paid to the government in the following year, are both included in the receipts of the following year. Cash basis reporting is preferred because it shows the amount of tax revenue actually available to a government. See also Accrual Basis Accounting.

Cash on Delivery (COD): Where small value goods are sent by Post Office Parcel or a courier and are released only after payment of the invoice plus COD charges.

Cash Reserve Ratio (CRR): See Reserve Bank of India, *191*.

Cash with Order (CWO): A payment in advance. CWO is usually used for small orders and for new buyers and may even be asked for before production begins.

Cashier's Cheque: A cheque drawn on the funds of the bank, not against the funds in a depositor's account. However, the depositor pays for the cashier's cheque with funds from his account. The primary benefit of a cashier's cheque is that the recipient of the cheque is assured that the funds are available.

Cease and Desist Letter: A letter requesting that a company stops the activity mentioned in the letter.

Central Bank: Central Bank of a country is usually a government owned and operated institution that controls the banking system and money supply in the economy. It has, *inter alia*, the following responsibilities: (a) issuing currency, (b) managing money supply, (c) administering rate of interest, (d) monitoring borrowing and lending policies of commercial banks, (e) undertaking governmental banking activities, and (f) maintaining foreign exchange reserves, external value of money and a country's balance of payments.

Central banks of the leading Western nations (Federal Reserve System in the US, Deutsche Bondsman in West Germany, Bank of Japan, and Bank of England) generally work closely to improve the global monetary system and to conduct varying degrees of co-ordinated currency support actions in times of severe exchange or other financial problems. See also Reserve Bank of India.

Certificate of Release: A certificate signed by a lender indicating that a mortgage has been fully paid and all debts satisfied.

Certificates of Deposit (CDs): CDs are essentially securitised short-term time deposits issued by banks during periods of tight liquidity, at relatively high interest rates (in comparison with term deposits). However, the transaction cost of CDs is often lower as compared with that of retail deposits. When credit picks up, placing pressure on banks' liquidity, banks try to meet their liquidity gap by issuing CDs, often at a premium. The required amounts are mobilised in larger amounts through CDs, often for short periods in order to avoid interest liability overhang in the subsequent months when credit demand slackens. As banks offer higher interest rates on CDs, subscribers find it profitable to hold CDs till maturity. As a result, the secondary market for CDs has been slow to develop.

Certified Cheque: A personal cheque drawn by an individual that is certified (guaranteed) to be good. The face of the cheque bears the words *certified* or *accepted*, and is signed by an official of the bank or thrift institution issuing the cheque. The signature signifies that: (a) the signature of the drawer is genuine, and (b) sufficient funds are on deposit and earmarked for payment of the cheque.

Change in Stock: At the beginning of a year, every enterprise possesses some stock of raw materials, half-finished goods and finished goods which could not be sold in the previous year. This is called opening stock. At the end of the year, it is left with some stock of intermediate goods or raw materials, semi-finished goods and finished goods. This is called closing stock. The difference between the opening stock and closing stock is the change in stocks. Change in stock = closing stock – opening stock.

Charge-off: The balance on a credit obligation that a lender no longer expects to be repaid and writes off as a bad debt.

Cheap Money: It is a situation in which credit is easily available at relatively low rate of interest.

Cheque: A written order instructing a financial institution to pay immediately on demand a specified amount of money from the cheque writer's account to the person named on the cheque or, if a specific person is not named, to whoever bears the cheque to the institution for payment.

Cheque Account: A demand deposit account subject to withdrawal of funds by cheque.

Cheque Truncation: The conversion of data on a cheque into an electronic image after a cheque enters the processing system. Cheque truncation eliminates the need to return cancelled cheques to customers.

Clean Bill of Lading: See Bill of Lading, *22*.

Clean Draft: It is a draft to which no documents have been attached.

Clean Float: Clean float refers to a system in which exchange rates are determined by market forces rather than government intervention or restrictions. See also Managed Float.

Closed-end Credit: Generally, any credit sale agreement in which the amount advanced, plus any finance charges, is expected to be repaid in full by a specified date. Most real estate and automobile loans are closed-end agreements. Also called closed-end loan.

Closed-end Loan: See Closed-end Credit, *36*.

Closing a Mortgage Loan: The consummation of a contractual real estate transaction in which all appropriate documents are signed and the proceeds of the mortgage loan are then disbursed by the lender.

Closing Costs: The expenses incurred by sellers and buyers in transferring ownership in real property. The costs of closing may include the origination fee, discount points, attorneys' fees, loan fees, title search and insurance, survey charge, recordation fees, and the credit report charge.

Collateral: Assets that are offered to secure a loan or other credit. For example, if you get a real estate mortgage, the bank's collateral is typically your house. Collateral becomes subject to seizure on default.

Collected Funds: Cash deposits or cheques that have been presented for payment and for which payment has been received.

Collection Agency: A company hired by a creditor to collect a debt that is owed. Creditors typically hire a collection agency only after they have made efforts to collect the debt themselves, usually through letters and telephone calls.

Collection Items: Items—such as drafts, notes, and acceptances—received for collection and credited to a depositor's account after payment has been received. Collection items are usually subject to special instructions and may involve additional fees. Most banks impose a special fee, called a collection charge, for handling collection items.

Collection Papers: All documents (invoices, bills of lading etc.) submitted to a buyer for the purpose of receiving payment for a shipment.

Co-maker: A person who signs a note to guarantee a loan made to another person and is jointly liable with the maker for repayment of the loan (also known as a co-signer).

Commercial Bank: A commercial bank is a financial intermediary which accepts deposits of money from the public and lends them with a view to make profits. A post office may accept deposits but it cannot be called a bank because it does not perform the other essential function of a bank, i.e. lending money. Similarly, some other institutions like Unit Trust of India (UTI) (q.v.) may be lending to others but since they do not accept deposits, they cannot be termed as banks. They are non-banking financial institutions.

The banking system forms the core of the financial sector of an economy. The role of commercial banks is particularly important in underdeveloped countries. Through mobilisation of resources and their better allocation, commercial banks play an important role in the development process of underdeveloped countries. By offering attractive saving schemes and ensuring safety of deposits, commercial banks encourage willingness to save among the people. By reaching out to people in rural areas, they help convert idle savings into effective ones. Commercial banks improve the allocation of resources by lending money to priority sectors of the economy. These banks provide a meeting ground for the savers and the investors. Savers may not invest either because of inadequate savings and/or lack of risk-taking spirit.

Functions of a Commercial Bank: A commercial bank generally performs the following functions.

1. It accepts deposits which are of various types like current, savings, recurring and fixed deposits.
2. It grants credit in various forms such as loans and advances, discounting of bills and investment in open market securities.
3. It collects cheques, drafts, bills and other instruments for its depositors.
4. It provides remittance facilities through drafts and telegraphic transfers.
5. It renders investment services such as underwriter and banker for new issues of securities to the public.
6. It provides such agency services as purchase and sale of foreign exchange, acceptance of tax payments, electricity bills etc.
7. It provides facilities like travellers' cheques, gift cheques and safe deposit vaults to its customers.

Balance Sheet of a Commercial Bank: Balance sheet of a bank is a statement of liabilities and assets of a bank at a point of time. It reflects the policies, size and soundness of the operations of a bank. The liabilities indicate the sources of its funds. The assets show the nature of its investments. To understand the conflict between liquidity and profitability and how it is resolved, the study of the balance sheet of a bank is necessary.

It is pertinent to note that a commercial bank has to satisfy the interests of three distinct groups.

1. Depositors whose withdrawal needs it must meet without delay.
2. Shareholders for whom it must earn profits.
3. Central bank under the control and supervision of which it has to work and abide by its various directives.

It is indeed a tightrope walking for the bank. How it tries to satisfy the three masters simultaneously will become clear with an understanding of its balance sheet.

***Liabilities of a Bank*:** The liabilities of a bank are mainly composed of the following items.

1. **Paid up Capital and Reserves:** Paid up capital means the amount of share capital actually contributed by the shareholders. Reserves are retained earnings or undistributed profits of the banks. These two items put together constitute the owned funds of the bank.
2. **Deposits:** Deposits from the public are the main source of funds for a commercial bank. Therefore, these deposits constitute the main liability of a bank. These deposits are of various types like current, savings and fixed deposits.
3. **Borrowings:** Commercial banks borrow from each other as well as from non-banking financial institutions like LIC, GIC, UTI.
4. **Miscellaneous:** Liabilities like bills payable.

***Assets of a Bank*:** The asset portfolio of a bank is of crucial importance. It strikes a balance between liquidity and profitability of a bank. A commercial bank has to earn profit for its shareholders and at the same time satisfy the withdrawal needs of its customers. A bank tries to achieve the twin conflicting objectives by selecting a diversified and balanced asset portfolio within the framework of the regulations of the central bank. The various items of its assets described below will show that some are more liquid than others. The more liquid the asset, the less profitable it is.

1. **Cash:** Cash-in-hand (also called vault cash) is held to meet the withdrawal needs of the depositors. Commercial banks also hold cash balances with the RBI. These balances are held

with the RBI under the statutory cash reserve ratio.

2. **Money at Call/Short Notice:** Commercial banks lend their surplus cash to each other and also to other financial institutions for short periods of time. This type of lending earns interest for the banks while maintaining liquidity at the same time.
3. **Investment in Securities:** Banks are required statutorily to invest a part of their assets in Government securities. These securities carry a low rate of interest but banks can borrow from the RBI against these securities. Thus, they provide return as well as liquidity to the bank.
4. **Loans and Advances:** Loans and advances constitute the main item of a bank's assets. They are also the main source of income for the banks. Loans are given in the form of overdrafts, term loans, and demand loans.

Thus, we see that a bank holds its assets in such a way that the requirements of liquidity and profitability are balanced. Liabilities are shown on the left side and assets on the right side of a balance sheet.

Classification of Commercial Banks in India: Commercial banks in India can be classified in a variety of ways.

***Scheduled and Non-scheduled Banks*:** A scheduled bank is one which is included in the second schedule of the Reserve Bank of India Act, 1934. Certain conditions are to be satisfied to be eligible for this as, for example, a bank must be a corporation and not a partnership or a single-owner firm. Scheduled banks enjoy certain facilities like borrowings from the RBI. In return, they have to meet certain obligations of RBI like, maintaining a part of their cash reserves with the RBI. Non-scheduled banks are disappearing from the banking scene and hence they are not important.

***Indian and Foreign Banks*:** Indian banks are those which are incorporated in India and have their head offices in India. Some big Indian banks have their branches in foreign countries. Foreign banks are incorporated in foreign countries with their head offices outside India. They are scheduled banks and generally specialise in the field of foreign exchange.

***Public Sector and Private Sector Banks*:** The Central Government entered the banking business with the nationalisation of the Imperial Bank of India (now the State Bank of India) in 1955. In 1969, 14 large banks were nationalised and again in 1980, 6 more banks were taken over by the Government. These nationalised banks are called public sector banks. The others are private sector banks.

Commercial Bill: It is a marketable instrument and an important device for providing short-term credit to business and industry. Commercial bills (or bills of exchange) are issued by business firms. Business firms often sell goods on credit and the buyers promise to pay the value of goods after a specified period of time, say 3 months. Thus, a bill with a maturity period of 3 months is like a post-dated cheque to be honoured by the buyer of goods. The holder of the bill may need cash before the maturity date and in that case he can sell it to some other person or to a bank at a discount. Bills are of two types: (a) demand bills which are payable on demand or presentation or sight as, for example, a bank draft, and (b) time bills which are payable after a stipulated time period, generally 3 months.

Commercial Invoice: It is a basic export document containing all the information which is required for preparing *all other* documents. It gives the description of the exporters and importers, their names and addresses, goods and their prices, terms and conditions and name of the shipping vessel. The description of the goods should tally fully with that given in the Letter of Credit (q.v.).

Commercial Paper (CP): It is privately placed with investors through the agency of banks. Banks act as both principals (i.e. as counter parties in purchases and sales) and agents in dealership and placement.

In India, CP was introduced as a money market instrument in January 1990. The purpose was to enable the companies to diversify their sourcing of short-term borrowings. It also provided investors with an additional instrument for investment. CP is issued by non-banking companies and All-India Financial Institutions (AIFIs) as an unsecured promissory note or in a dematerialised form at a rate of discount not tied to any transaction.

The pricing of CP usually lies between the scheduled commercial banks' lending rate and some representative money market rate. The Indian CP market is driven by the demand for CP by scheduled commercial banks, which in turn is governed by bank liquidity. Banks' investments in CP, despite a positive interest rate differential between the bank loan rate and the CP rate, may be explained by two factors, viz.: (i) the higher transaction costs of bank loans, and (ii) the relative profitability of CP as an attractive short-term instrument to park funds during times of high liquidity.

As inter-bank call rates are typically lower than the CP rates, some banks also fund CP by borrowing from the call money market and thus book profit through arbitrage between the two money markets. Most of the CPs seem to have been issued by the manufacturing companies for a maturity period of approximately 3 months or less, mainly due to the fact that investors do not wish to lock funds for long periods of time.

Commercial Policy: It refers to a country's official policy towards foreign trade, tariffs, quotas and non-tariff barriers. It also deals with the composition and direction of a country's foreign trade.

Commercial Treaty: It is an agreement between two or more countries setting forth the conditions under which business between the countries may be transacted. It covers, *inter alia*, tariff privileges, terms on which property may be owned, and the manner in which claims may be settled.

Commodity Agreements: These are agreements among producer countries of primary products (sugar, copper, coffee, cocoa, tin etc.) to control prices and export volumes in the world market. Under such agreements, export quota of each member country is fixed. However, problems arise in the implementation of such agreements when signatory countries do not stick to their quota or do not agree on the quota allotted to them.

Compliance Risk: It is defined as the risk of legal or regulatory sanctions, as a result of an entity's failure to comply with laws, regulations, rules, and codes of conduct applicable.

Confirmed Letter of Credit: See Letter of Credit, *141*.

Conglomerate: It refers to production units selling unrelated products which are united into one big business firm.

Consignee: It means the person or firm named in a freight contract to whom goods have been consigned or turned over. For export control purposes, the documentation differentiates between an *intermediate* consignee and an *ultimate* consignee.

Consignment: It refers to delivery of merchandise from an exporter (the consignor) to an agent (the consignee) under agreement that the agent sells the merchandise for the account of the exporter. The consignor retains title to the goods until sold. The consignee sells the goods for commission and remits the net proceeds to the consignor.

Co-operative Banks: Co-operative banks in India are more than 100 years old. These banks came into existence with the enactment of the Agricultural Credit Co-operative Societies Act in 1904. Co-operative banks form an integral part of the banking system in India. These banks operate mainly for the benefit of rural areas, particularly the agricultural sector. Co-operative banks mobilise deposits and supply agricultural and rural credit with a wider outreach. They are the main source of institutional credit to the farmers. Co-operative banks are chiefly responsible for breaking the monopoly of moneylenders in providing credit to agriculturists. They have also been an important instrument for various development schemes, particularly subsidy-based programmes for the poor. Co-operative banks operate for non-agricultural sector also but their role is small.

Though much smaller as compared to scheduled commercial banks, co-operative banks constitute an important segment of the Indian banking system. They have an extensive branch network and reach out to people in remote areas. They have traditionally played an important role in creating banking habits among the lower and middle-income groups and in strengthening the rural credit delivery system.

Unfortunately, financial reforms have not impacted the functioning of co-operative banks. This was brought out clearly in the following observation of the Reserve Bank of India, "Since the introduction of reforms, there has been very little perceptible improvement in either stability or efficiency of co-operative banks. In particular, the asset quality and profitability of scheduled Urban Co-operative Banks (UCBs) showed some deterioration in the reform period. Positive impact of reforms, as has been witnessed in the case of commercial banking sector, may take longer to get manifested for co-operative banks given the late start of the reform process in this sector."

The financial reforms process initiated in 1991 has tried to achieve regulatory convergence among various financial intermediaries in view of their systemic importance. Therefore, the basic objectives and instruments of reforms for co-operative banks have been the same as for State Co-operative Banks (SCBs). However, given the special characteristics of co-operative banks, they have been extended certain dispensations in terms of pace and sequencing of reforms.

The co-operative banking system forms an integral part of the Indian financial system. The co-operative banking structure in India comprises urban co-operative banks and rural co-operative credit institutions.

Corporate Debt Restructuring: A Special Group (Chairperson: Smt. S. Gopinath) was appointed by RBI to undertake a further review of the corporate debt restructuring (CDR) mechanism and suggest certain changes/improvements in the existing scheme for enhancing its scope and to make it more efficient. In pursuance of the recommendations made by the Special Group, major modifications were proposed in the draft guidelines issued on May 6, 2005 in the existing CDR scheme which included the following.

1. Extension of scheme to corporate entities where banks and institutions have an outstanding exposure of ₹ 10 crore or more from the earlier exposure of ₹ 20 crore and above.
2. Requirement of support of 60 percent of creditors by number in addition to the support of 75 percent of creditors by value with a view to making the decision-making process more equitable.
3. Linking the restoration of asset classification prevailing on the date of reference to CDR Cell for implementation of package within three months from the date of approval of the package.
4. Restricting the regulatory concession in asset classification and provisioning requirement to the first restructuring where the package also has to meet certain norms relating to turnaround period and minimum sacrifice and funds infusion by promoters.
5. Convergence in the methodology for computation of economic sacrifice among banks and FIs.
6. Regulatory treatment of non-SLR instruments acquired while funding interest or in *lieu* of outstanding principal and valuation of such instruments.
7. Limiting the RBI's role to providing broad guidelines for the CDR system.
8. Enhancing balance sheet disclosures.
9. Pro-rata sharing of additional finance requirement.
10. Including one-time settlement (OTS) as part of the CDR scheme to make the exit option more flexible.
11. Discretion to the core group in dealing with wilful defaulters in certain cases.

Corporate Income Tax: It is levied on the earnings of corporations. A corporation (or a company) is regarded as a separate entity for purposes of income tax. Total income of a corporation is arrived at with reference to its profits shown in its profit and loss account. To such profits (or losses) are added those expenses which, though actually incurred by a corporation, are disallowed, partially or wholly, under the law. From this total, the amount of tax concessions is deducted to arrive at the taxable income of a corporation. Rate structure of corporation tax may be progressive or proportional depending upon the tax policy of a country.

Corporation Tax: See Corporate Income Tax, *46*.

Co-signer: An individual who signs the note of another person as support for the credit of the primary signer and who becomes responsible for the obligation (also known as a co-maker).

Cost and Freight (C and F): It is a price quotation that includes the cost of merchandise and freight charges for its shipment to a given destination. It does not include insurance of the shipment so that the buyer rather than the seller is responsible for any damage occurring during transit. See also Cost, Insurance and Freight.

Cost, Insurance and Freight (CIF): It is a price quotation that includes cost of merchandise, shipping insurance and freight charges to a specific destination. It is generally applied to imports to work out their prices. See also Cost and Freight

Credit: By credit we mean finance made available by a lender to a borrower. The personal resources of an entrepreneur are generally inadequate to undertake production on large-scale. He needs credit to start production and use modern technology. There are various classifications of credit, each with its own significance.

Sources of Credit: Credit may be classified on the basis of who provides it? Sources of credit can be divided into two categories: (a) institutional sources, and (b) non-institutional sources. Institutional sources are further sub-divided into: (i) banking sources (commercial banks), and (ii) non-banking sources (e.g. Unit Trust of India). Non-institutional sources include moneylenders, relatives, friends and other private parties.

End-uses of Credit: Credit may be classified on the basis of the use to which it is put. The two main categories of end-uses are: (a) production, and (b) consumption. The production category is further sub-divided into: (i) industry, (ii) agriculture, and (iii) trade.

Period of Credit: Credit may be classified term-wise into the following categories: (a) short-term credit, i.e. credit for a period of 1 year or less, (b) medium-term credit, i.e. credit for more than a year but less than 5 years, and (c) long-term credit, i.e. credit for a period of more than 5 years.

Credit Card Account Agreement: A written agreement that explains: (a) terms and conditions of the account, (b) credit usage and payment by the cardholder, and (c) duties and responsibilities of the card issuer.

Credit Card Issuer: Any financial institution that issues bank cards to those who apply for them.

Credit Default Swap (CDS): See Credit Derivatives, *47*.

Credit Derivatives: The credit derivatives are gaining increasing popularity in many countries. Since the early 1990s, there has been proliferation of different types of credit derivatives in several countries.

A credit derivative is a contract (derivative) to transfer the risk of the total return on a credit asset falling below an agreed level, without transfer of the underlying asset. This is usually achieved by transferring risk on a credit reference asset. Early forms of credit derivatives were financial guarantees. Credit derivatives are designed to allow independent trading/hedging of credit risk. It is also possible to transfer and/or transform credit risk through securitisation. Credit derivative is a logical extension of two of the most significant developments in financial markets, *viz.*, securitisation and derivatives.

Forms of Credit Derivatives: Credit derivatives are instruments that transfer a part or all of the credit risk of an obligation (or a pool of obligations), without transferring the ownership of the underlying asset(s). This is usually achieved by transferring risk on a credit reference asset. Three common forms of credit derivatives are credit default swap (CDS), total return swap (TRS) and credit linked note (CLN).

A. Credit Default Swap (CDS): A CDS consists of swapping, usually on an ongoing basis, the risk premium inherent in an interest rate on a bond or a loan in return for a cash payment that is made in the event of default by the debtor. The CDS has become the main driver of the credit derivatives market, offering liquid price discovery and trading on which the rest of the market is based. It is an agreement between a protection buyer and a protection seller, whereby the buyer pays a periodic fee in return for a contingent payment by the seller upon a credit event happening in the reference entity. The contingent payment usually replicates the loss incurred by creditor of the reference entity in the event of its default. It covers only the credit risk embedded in the asset, risks arising from other factors, such as interest rate movements, remain with the buyer.

B. Total Return Swap (TRS): A TRS (also known as total rate of return swap) is a contract between two counterparties, whereby they swap periodic payments for the period of the contract. Typically, one party receives the total return (interest payments plus any capital gains or losses for the payment period) from a specified reference asset, while the other receives a specified fixed or floating cash flow that is not related to the creditworthiness of the reference asset, as with a vanilla interest rate swap. The payments are based upon the same notional amount. The reference asset may be any asset, index or basket of assets. The TRS is simply a mechanism that allows one party to derive the economic benefit of owning an asset without use of the balance sheet, and which allows the other to effectively; buy protection; against loss in value due to ownership of a credit assets.

While the CDS provides protection against specific credit events, the TRS protects against the loss of value irrespective of cause, whether default and widening of credit spreads, among others.

C. Credit Linked Note (CLN): A CLN is an instrument whose cash flow depends upon a credit event, which can be a default, credit spread, or rating change. The definition of the relevant credit events must be negotiated by the parties to the note. A CLN, in effect, combines a credit-default swap with a regular note (with coupon, maturity, redemption). Given its regular-note features, a CLN is an on-balance sheet asset, unlike a CDS.

Significance of Credit Derivatives: Credit derivative markets are most active where credit quality measurement and rating systems are transparent and have widespread adoption as in North America and Europe. In addition, the demand for structured credit products in Asia and the Middle East has been growing. The rapid pace of growth and widespread participation in the credit derivatives market in several countries has transformed the financial landscape. Credit derivatives have significance for both banks and investors in mitigating credit risk. For instance, a commercial bank can use credit derivatives to manage the risk of its loan portfolio and an investment bank can use credit derivatives to manage the risks it incurs when underwriting securities. Investors—such as an insurance company, asset manager, or hedge fund—can use credit derivatives to align its credit risk exposure with its desired credit risk profile.

Credit derivatives in international markets have effectively helped to enhance the efficiency of the financial system by providing to both bank and non-bank financial institutions access to a broader range of risk-return combinations and a wider pool of underlying risks and enhancing the liquidity of corporate bond markets. The information revealed through credit derivative mechanism is very useful for supervision and market surveillance.

Benefits of Credit Derivatives: Banks and the financial institutions derive at least three main benefits from credit derivatives:

Credit derivatives allow banks to transfer credit risk and hence free up capital, which can be used for other productive purposes.

Banks can conduct business on existing client relationships in excess of exposure norms and transfer away the risks. For instance, a bank which has hit its exposure limits with a client group may have to turn down a lucrative guarantee deal. However, with credit derivatives, the bank can take up the guarantee and maintain its exposure limits by transferring the credit risk on the guarantee or previous exposures. This allows bank to maintain client relationships.

Banks can construct and manage a credit risk portfolio of their own choice and risk appetite unconstrained by funds, distribution and sales effort.

Risks Involved in Credit Derivatives: Credit derivatives pose risk management challenges of their own. Credit derivatives can transform credit risk in intricate ways that may not be easy to understand. Complex credit derivatives rely on complex models, leading to model risk. Credit rating agencies interpret this complexity for investors, but their ratings can be misunderstood, creating rating agency risk. The settlement of a credit derivative contract following a default can have its own complications, creating settlement risk. Apart from these risks, the credit risk remains the core risk in the credit derivative segment. The use of credit derivative instruments has changed the underlying borrower-lender relationship and established new relationships between lenders that become risk shedders and the new risk takers. This new relationship has the potential for market failure due, for instance, to asymmetric information. The growth of hedge funds, particularly credit-oriented hedge funds, has accelerated market development and credit risk dispersion. While credit derivative markets increasingly facilitate the primary transfer of credit risk, secondary market liquidity is still lacking within some segments, creating the potential for market disruptions. As such, these markets are subject to increased attention from supervisors and policymakers and raise some supervisory concerns.

In short, the use of credit derivatives raises the following concerns:

1. Some of the credit derivatives, which are being used, are at their infancy and need to mature. Introduction of such products, therefore, may be potentially destabilising.
2. The measurement and management of credit risk is much more complicated than market risk.
3. Documentation risk is an important aspect of credit derivatives.

Certain incentive issues arise with the use of credit derivatives. This is because such instruments typically change the underlying borrower-lender relationship and establish new relationships between lenders that become risk shedders and the new risk takers. This new relationship has the potential for market failure due, for instance, to asymmetric information. See also Financial Derivatives.

Credit Disability Insurance: A type of insurance, also known as accident and health insurance that makes payments on the loan if one falls become ill or is injured and cannot work.

Credit Guarantee Corporation (CGC): CGC was promoted by RBI as a public limited company in 1971. The main thrust of the credit guarantee schemes introduced by the CGC was to encourage the commercial banks to meet the credit needs of the hitherto neglected sectors, particularly the weaker sections of the society engaged in non-industrial activities.

In 1978, CGC was merged, along with Deposit Insurance Corporation (DIC) (q.v.), to form the Deposit Insurance and Credit Guarantee Corporation of India (DICGC) (q.v.).

Credit Information Bureau (India) Limited (CIBIL): Set up in 2000, it provides a vital service, which allows its members to make informed, objective and faster credit decisions. CIBIL's aim is to fulfil the need of credit granting institutions for comprehensive credit information by collecting, collating and disseminating credit information pertaining to both commercial and consumer borrowers, to a closed user group of members. Banks, financial institutions, non-banking financial companies, housing finance companies and credit card companies use CIBIL's services. Data sharing is based on the principle of reciprocity, which means that only members who have submitted all their credit data, may access credit information reports from CIBIL.

With a view to strengthening the legal mechanism and facilitating credit information companies to collect, process and share credit information on borrowers of banks/FIs, a draft Credit Information Companies (Regulation) Bill was passed in May 2005 and notified in June 2005. The Government and the Reserve Bank have framed rules and regulations for implementation of the Act, with specific provisions for protecting individual borrower's rights and obligations. The rules and regulations were notified on December 14, 2006. In terms of the provisions of the Act, after obtaining the certificate of registration from the Reserve Bank to commence/carry on business of credit information companies will be able to collect all types of credit information (positive as well as negative) from their member credit institutions and disseminate the same in the form of credit reports to the specified users/individuals.

Credit Life Insurance: A type of life insurance that helps repay a loan if one should die before the loan is fully repaid. This is optional coverage.

Credit Limit: The maximum amount of credit that is available on a credit card or other line of credit account.

Credit Linked Note (CLN): See Credit Derivatives, *47*.

Credit Rating: It is a rating classification in respect of credit worthiness of companies, public institutions and countries. AAA symbol indicates highest degree of commercial integrity with minimal risk of default. Other credit ratings in descending order of commercial integrity are: AA, A, BBB, BB, B etc. These ratings are awarded by Standard and Poor's or by Moody's, the two main rating companies of US. The four major credit rating agencies in India are: Credit Rating Information Services of India Ltd. (CRISIL), Investment Information and Credit Rating Agency Ltd. (ICRA), Fitch India Ratings Pvt. Ltd., and Credit Analysis and Research Ltd. (CARE).

Crowding-out: The term is descriptive of any group/section being pushed out of a market. In the context of financial market, the demand for credit by the government and other public sector institutions may be so strong and inflexible that credit requirements of households and companies are crowded-out.

CRR: See Cash Reserve Ratio, *33*.

Cum Bonus and Ex Bonus: Cum bonus means *with bonus,* i.e. a quotation of a share where the right to bonus is transferred to the buyer. Ex bonus means *without the attached right to the bonus just announced,* i.e. the market quotation of a share where such a right is retained by the seller.

Cum Dividend and Ex Dividend: Cum dividend means *with dividend*, i.e. market quotation of a share where the right to receive the dividend immediately due is transferred to the buyer. Ex dividend means *without the attached right to the dividend just due*, i.e. a market quotation of a share where such a right to dividend is retained by the seller.

Cum Interest and Ex Interest: Cum interest means *with interest,* i.e. market quotation of an interest bearing security where the right to receive the interest payment immediately due is transferred to the buyer. Ex interest means *without the attached right to interest just due,* i.e. the market quotation of a debenture where such interest on it is retained by the seller.

Cum Rights and Ex Rights: Cum rights means *with rights,* i.e. market quotation of a share where the benefit of rights issue offered by the company is transferred to the buyer. Ex rights means *without the attached rights to new shares issued by the company,* i.e. market quotation of a share where such rights are retained by the seller.

Currency: It means the monetary unit in use in a country. The term has different connotations.

Hard Currency: It refers to currency with full and easy convertibility and its conversion taking place at a nearly stable exchange rate and without any control of the country's monetary authorities to which that currency belongs. The assumption here is that the country concerned has a large foreign exchange reserve and a surplus in balance of payments. It is sometimes referred to as convertible currency.

Soft Currency: It is a currency with limited convertibility.

Inside and Outside Currencies: Currencies of member countries of an economic grouping are known as inside currencies while those of non-members are called outside currencies.

Exotic Currency: It refers to currency not having a developed international market and which is infrequently dealt with.

Currency Area: It refers to a group of countries having close economic and political ties and whose exchange rates are keyed to each other and are usually defined in terms of one currency of the group. They float as a group with respect to the rest of the world. This arrangement is a compromise between fixed and floating rates.

Currency Band: This refers to the maximum permitted range of fluctuations of a given currency against a reference currency.

Currency Clause: It is a clause is an export contract which specifies that the foreign currency (say pound sterling) payable for the goods shall vary in line with the market exchange rate of the local currency (say rupee) so as to maintain a constant (rupee) value of exports.

Currency Convertibility: It is of various kinds.

External Convertibility: It is a situation where convertibility is enjoyed solely by non-residents.

Internal Convertibility: Under it, conversion of a currency is permitted only for the residents of the country.

Partial Convertibility: If conversion of a currency is applicable only in terms of certain other currencies or only for certain transactions (mostly on current account of balance of payments) or only for a few institutions or persons, it is considered to have only partial convertibility.

Currency Fluctuations: Changes in the value of one currency relative to another. An exporter can protect against loss caused by fluctuating currencies during the sales contract period by taking out a forward exchange contract with a bank. The exporter, invoicing a buyer in a foreign currency for payment at an agreed future date, sells those expected receipts to a bank in advance (i.e. forward) of the due date of payment. The bank agrees to buy at a pre-determined forward rate of exchange which varies according to the time of future delivery, for example, one, three or six months, or longer. No money is exchanged at the time the forward contract is made, but under its terms the exporter is guaranteed a certain rate of exchange.

Current Account Convertibility: Current account convertibility allows residents to make and receive trade-related payments, i.e. receive foreign currency for export of goods and services and pay foreign currency for import of goods and services like travels, medical treatment and studies abroad. In other words, it permits free inflows and outflows for all purposes other than for capital purposes. Current account convertibility was introduced in India in August 1994 with the acceptance of the obligations under Article VIII of the IMF's Articles of Agreement. This drastic measure contributed significantly to boost India's exports. Presently, there is almost full convertibility on the current account and partial convertibility on the capital account. See also Capital Account Convertibility.

Current and Capital Transfers: Transfers made from the current income of the payer and added to the current income of the recipient for consumption expenditure are called current transfers. Capital transfers are defined as transfers in cash and in kind made out of the wealth/savings of the donor for the purpose of capital formation by the recipient.

Current Assets: See Asset, *8*.

Customs Bond: A bond that, in certain circumstances, importers must post to effect the entry of imported goods. A customs bond usually must be guaranteed by an approved surety. The bond acts as a security in order to ensure the collection of duties and taxes owed on imports and to facilitate compliance with other importation requirements.

Customs Duty: A tax on the import and export of goods levied by a national government and payable to it when the goods cross the customs boundaries of the nation. Hence, it is also called border tax. The term customs duty as an English expression originated in England during a period of disagreement between the king and the parliament over the king's right to collect it. King's supporters claimed that the sovereign had been vested with the authority to impose this levy by a long established custom. Hence, it is suggested that the term customs duty was derived. The right was claimed on the ground that customs duties were a reasonable return to the king for the protection and security he was supposed to provide on land and sea.

Customs duties are probably the most ancient form of taxation. They are as old as international trade itself. Just as domestic production flows provide the base for excise taxation, so also international trade flows are the basis for customs duties. These duties are levied either on *ad valorem* basis (i.e. as a percentage of the value of goods imported or exported) or on specific basis (i.e. as a stated amount per unit of weight, volume etc.). Customs duties can be classified into two categories: import duties, and export duties.

Import Duty: It is levied on the domestic value of the imported goods calculated at the official exchange rate. There are two main purposes of import duty: (a) to raise revenue for the government (revenue tariff), and (b) to discourage imports in order to protect a nation's domestic industry (protective tariff) or to correct disequilibrium (deficit) in its balance of payments. Other measures to protect indigenous industries from foreign competition are import licensing, import quotas, and outright import ban.

Export Duty: It is levied on export values expressed in domestic currency. Export duties can become an important source of revenue when a country enjoys comparatively strong position in respect of certain goods in the international market. Thus, when there is considerable disparity between the domestic and international prices of certain goods, levy of export duties is justified to mop up a part of the profits of exporters. Export duty on an item is levied after considering such factors as domestic production, likely exportable surpluses, demand for the item in the foreign markets, changes in exchange rates, and prices prevailing in the international market.

Cut-off Time: A time of day established by a bank for receipt of deposits. After the cut-off time, deposits are considered received on the next banking day.

Dd

Data Dissemination: It refers to all the means by which data are made available to the public, including dissemination on the Internet.

Data Warehouse: It means a large database of customer transactions, updated regularly, which is used as a source of information for data mining.

Dear Money: It refers to the policy of monetary restraint followed by the central bank of a country. By raising rate of interest and through other means, the central bank tries to reduce credit supply in order to relieve inflationary pressures in the economy.

Debit: A debit may be an account entry representing money you owe a lender or money that has been taken from your deposit account.

Debit Card: A debit card allows the account holder to access his funds electronically. Debit cards may be used to obtain cash from automated teller machines or purchase goods or services using point-of-sale systems. The use of a debit card involves immediate debiting and crediting of a consumer's account.

Debt Equity Ratio: It is calculated by dividing all debt by all equity capital of a company.

Debt Recovery Tribunals (DRTs): DRTs were set up under the Recovery of Debts Due to Banks and Financial Institutions Act, 1993 for expeditious adjudication and recovery of debts due to banks and financial institutions.

Debt Securities: The term covers all tradable securities, except those classified as equity securities. Debt securities include bonds, debentures, notes etc., money market or negotiable debt instruments.

Debt to Net-worth Ratio: It is the ratio of the total liabilities of a company to its net worth.

Debt Trap: It is a situation in which a government is unable to repay its past loans without fresh borrowings.

Debtor/Creditor Principle: There are two principles that may serve as the basis for geographic allocation of direct investment financial flows: the debtor/creditor principle and the Transactor Principle (q.v.). Under the debtor/creditor principle, transactions resulting from changes in financial claims of the compiling economy are allocated to the country or residence of the non-resident debtor, and transactions resulting in changes in financial liabilities are allocated to the country of residence of the non-resident creditor, even if the amounts are paid to or received from a different country.

Debt-to-income Ratio (DTI): The percentage of a consumer's monthly gross income that goes toward paying debts. Generally, the higher the ratio, the higher the perceived risk. Loans with higher risk are generally priced at a higher interest rate.

Declining-balance Depreciation Method: This depreciation method allows larger deductions in the early years of the useful life of an asset and smaller deductions towards the later years. The depreciation allowed is computed by multiplying a fixed rate by the asset's book value. Unlike the historical cost, the asset's book value declines from year to year by the amount of depreciation accumulated in earlier years. See also Straight-line Depreciation Method.

Deductions: Deductions mean all amounts which are eligible for subtraction from gross receipts of a business. Strictly speaking, a deduction relates to an actual outlay, e.g. expenditure on travelling. Tax laws must clearly specify as to which sums are allowed as deductions from gross receipts in order to determine the amount on which a given set of rates is to be applied.

Thus, a taxpayer is allowed, as a matter of practice, to deduct from his gross receipts the expenditures incurred to earn income. Since the net income basis of income tax is universally accepted, expenses related to producing or receiving income (i.e. income production costs) must be allowed as deductions from gross receipts. That the income tax should be based on a net income concept is necessary because if a gross concept is adopted, the tax would fall partly on expenditure (for earning income) instead of exclusively on income. It is the net income which represents ability-to-pay taxes.

Which expenditures are really incurred in connection with income production and to what extent they should be allowed as deductions from gross receipts are baffling questions for the tax designers. Familiar examples are the entertainment expenses of companies and the use of company cars. It is often difficult to identify such expenses and even if it is possible to do so, problems arise in deciding whether they were personal or related to business. Income tax laws generally elaborate allowable and disallowable deductions.

Deferred Payment: A payment postponed until a future date.

Delinquency: A debt that was not paid when due.

Demand Deposit: A deposit of funds that can be withdrawn without any advance notice.

Deposit Insurance and Credit Guarantee Corporation of India (DICGC): In 1978, two organizations—Deposit Insurance Corporation (DIC) (q.v.) and Credit Guarantee Corporation (CGC) (q.v.)—were merged to form DICGC with the twin objectives of giving protection to small bank depositors and providing guarantee cover to credit facilities extended to certain categories of small borrowers belonging to the weaker sections of society. DICGC is a wholly-owned subsidiary of the RBI.

Deposit Insurance Corporation (DIC): A wholly-owned subsidiary of the RBI, it commenced operations in 1962. A number of important developments concerning deposit insurance took place during 1967-81. The DIC Act was amended in 1968 to extend the insurance scheme to deposits with cooperative banks. This phase witnessed strong growth and consolidation of the deposit insurance fund consequent upon the expansion of bank deposits and progressive increase in the coverage of insured deposits. In 1978, DIC was merged, along with Credit Guarantee Corporation (CGC) (q.v.), to form the Deposit Insurance and Credit Guarantee Corporation of India (DICGC) (q.v.).

Deposit Insurance System

India was the second country to institute a Deposit Insurance Scheme way back in 1961 in the wake of failure of a few banks. The deposit insurance system is designed to provide protection to small depositors who lack adequate financial skills and do not have the wherewithal to monitor their banks. The scheme is in the nature of a pay-box system in the case of: (a) liquidation, and (b) reconstruction/amalgamation of an insured bank.

The scheme is operated by Deposit Insurance and Credit Guarantee Corporation of India (DICGC) (q.v.).

In India, deposit insurance is compulsory for all banks. All deposits—with the exception of deposits of foreign governments, deposits of State/Central Governments, inter-bank deposits, and deposits held abroad—are insured by the DICGC.

DICGC's liability to the depositors of an insured bank arises in the event of the liquidation of that bank or its amalgamation with another bank or its reconstruction, and the claim payment needs to be made before the expiry of two months from the receipt of the claim.

With a view to educating the small depositors, DICGC has taken steps to increase public awareness of the deposit insurance scheme by sending relevant written materials to the insured banks for them to display in all branches at all places where depositor interaction is involved. DICGC has also hosted its own website (www.dicgc.org.in) for providing information to the public.

Deposit Slip: It is an itemized memorandum of the cash and other funds that a customer presents to the bank for credit to his/her account.

Depreciation: Every producing enterprise possesses, at the beginning of the year, a certain amount of fixed capital in the form of buildings, machines and equipment. During the year, fixed capital goes down in value due to normal wear and tear which is not made good by current repairs and maintenance. Its value may also go down by foreseen obsolescence. Loss of value due to normal wear and tear and expected obsolescence is called *depreciation* or consumption of fixed capital or capital consumption. However, loss of value due to unforeseen (unexpected) obsolescence, natural calamities (floods, fires and earthquakes), thefts etc. is not depreciation. It is called *capital loss*. Annual depreciation allowance represents a charge against current year's production. Estimation of depreciation assumes significance because in a dynamic economy technological progress may necessitate the replacement of a fixed asset before the expiry of its physical life.

Depreciation estimation poses both conceptual and statistical problems. Depreciation is normally estimated on the basis of the expected life of the fixed capital and the interest rate, rather than on the basis of actual current capital consumption. It is very difficult to estimate correctly the life of a capital equipment. Wear and tear differs from machine to machine and from firm to firm. Therefore, it is calculated either as a fixed percentage of: (a) gross value of output, or (b) of invested capital. The second method, commonly used in business practice, yields more stable annual allowance.

In international trade, the term depreciation refers to the fall in the free market value of domestic currency in terms of foreign currencies.

Depression: It is a prolonged period of low economic activities with high unemployment in an economy.

Deregulation: Lifting of government controls over an industry.

Derivatives: See Credit Derivatives, *47;* and Financial Derivatives, *82*.

Devaluation: As part of a government's commercial policy, it refers to deliberate reduction in the value of domestic currency in relation to foreign currencies. Devaluation makes domestically produced goods cheaper for the foreigners and foreign goods expensive for the locals. Hence, imports are reduced and exports are promoted to improve the trade balance. For successful devaluation, it is necessary that demand for imports as well as exports is relatively elastic.

Development Finance Institutions (DFIs): DFIs or simply financial institutions were set up in India at various points of time starting from the late 1940s to cater to the medium to long-term financing requirements of industry as the capital market in India had not developed sufficiently. After Independence in 1947, the national government adopted the path of planned economic development and launched the First Five Year Plan in 1951. This strategy of development provided the critical inducement for establishment of DFIs at both all-India and state-levels. In order to perform their role, DFIs were extended funds of the RBI and government guaranteed bonds, which constituted major sources of their funds. Funds from these sources were not only available at concessional rates, but also on a long-term basis with their maturity period ranging from 10-15 years. On the asset side, their operations were marked by near absence of competition.

A large variety of financial institutions have come into existence over the years to perform various types of financial activities. While some of them operate at all-India level, others are state level institutions. Besides providing direct loans (including rupee loans, foreign currency loans), financial institutions also extend financial assistance by way of underwriting and direct subscription and by issuing guarantees.

Recently, some DFIs have started extending short-term/working capital finance, although term-lending continues to be their primary activity.

Direct Deposit: A payment that is electronically deposited into an individual's account at a depository institution.

Direct Tax: It is a tax the ultimate burden of which falls on the person on whom it is levied. In other words, it is a tax that cannot be shifted from the original payer to someone else. It is contrasted with Indirect Tax (q.v.) which can readily be shifted to ultimate consumers of the commodity or service taxed. John Stuart Mill, the celebrated British economist of the nineteenth century, distinguished between direct and indirect taxes as follows. "A direct tax is one which is demanded from the very person who, it is intended or desired, should pay it. Indirect taxes are those which are demanded from one person in the expectation and intention that he shall indemnify himself at the expense of another."

Income tax, property tax, and payroll tax are generally considered direct taxes, although many economists believe that it is possible to pass on these taxes under certain circumstances. Corporate income tax, a supposedly direct tax, is known to be shifted to consumers in many countries. Direct taxes, though administratively inconvenient, are preferred because they: (a) can be related to ability-to-pay, (b) satisfy the principle of certainty, and (c) create civic consciousness.

Dirty Float: See Managed Float, *148*.

Disclosures: Certain information that Federal and State laws require creditors to give to borrowers relative to the terms of the credit extended.

Dividend: It is the payment authorised by the board of directors of a company for pro rata distribution among the shares outstanding. On preference shares, it is generally a fixed amount. On common shares, the dividend varies with the fortunes of the company.

Dividend Cover: It is the ratio of the dividend paid to the net profit out of which it is paid.

Dividend to Price Ratio: It is the ratio of the dividend per share paid by a company to the market price of one share of that company. For example, a dividend of ₹ 1.50 per share with a market price of ₹ 30 gives a dividend yield of 1.50/30 x 100 = 5 percent.

Document Collections: The term stipulates that the exporter ships goods to the importer without a letter of credit or another form of guaranteed payment. The importer must sign a sight draft before receiving the necessary documents to pick up the goods.

Documentary Bill: It is used when the seller of goods to a customer abroad wishes to obtain payment or some form of security before the goods are actually delivered. The seller will draw a bill on the consignee for the value of the goods, and will attach to it the copy of the invoice, the insurance policy and the Bills of Lading (q.v.). These documents will be handed to his banker, who in turn will forward them to his own correspondent at the place where the consignee of the goods is at sea. When this is done, the bank will require a letter of hypothecation empowering it to sell the goods in the event of default by the consignor.

Documentary Letter of Credit (DLC): A document issued by a bank which guarantees the payment of a customer's drafts for a specified period and up to a specified amount. DLC provides a more secure means of carrying out transactions in import-export trade than by documentary bills collection. A letter of credit when transmitted through a bank, usually in the exporter's country, becomes the means by which the exporter obtains payment. The necessary documents, correctly completed, are presented to a bank by an agreed date. If the terms of the credit are met, an exporter can receive payment from a bank immediately.

Door-step Banking: In May 1983, banks were advised by the RBI not to extend any banking facilities at the premises of their customers without obtaining its prior permission. Several requests, however, were received from Government Departments such as Railways requesting to make available banking services including collection of cash at their premises. Keeping this and representations from certain banks in view, it was decided in April 2005 that a scheme for providing services at the premises of a customer within the framework of Section 23 of the Banking Regulation Act, 1949 may be formulated by banks with the approval of their Boards and submitted to the RBI for approval. In order to ensure that Central and State Government departments are not inconvenienced, agency banks in the interregnum may continue to lift cash and collect credit instruments from their premises.

Double Tax Treaty: It means a convention or an agreement among countries for the avoidance of double taxation of income and capital and bringing uniformity in the allocation of taxation rights in cross-border situations. It is essentially a bargain between two treaty countries as regards the division of tax revenue between them in respect of income falling to be taxed in both jurisdictions. Since treaty negotiations involve bargaining, each side seeks concessions from the other and it is not necessary that strict *quid pro quo* is achieved at the end.

Double Taxation: It refers to the application of two separate taxes or tax systems to the same tax base, e.g. income. Double taxation (or tax duplication) occurs when the same base is assessed twice either by the same tax jurisdiction or by two competing tax jurisdictions either at different levels of government in a country or at the same level of government in different countries.

Double Taxation Relief: It is an arrangement to prevent the same income from being taxed twice, particularly when a shareholder and a company are domiciled in different countries. See also Double Taxation.

Draft: A signed, written order by which one party (the drawer) instructs another party (the drawee) to pay a specified sum to a third party (the payee), at sight or at a specific date. Typical bank drafts are negotiable instruments and are similar in many ways to cheques.

Draft Bill of Exchange: A written, unconditional order for payment from one person (the drawer) to another (the drawee). It directs the drawee to pay a specified sum of money, in a given currency, at a specific date to the drawer. A sight draft calls for immediate payment (on sight) while a time draft calls for payments at a readily determined future date.

Drawee: The person (or bank) who is expected to pay a cheque or draft when it is presented for payment.

Drawee Bank: The bank upon which a cheque is drawn.

Drawer: The individual or firm that issues or signs a draft and thus stands to receive payment of the indicated amount from the drawee.

Duty Drawback: It refers to repayment of import duty, partially or fully, to exporters of commodities in the manufacture of which imported materials and components are used. Duty drawback scheme is a device to encourage exports. Most often, the scheme is used for imported raw materials or semi-finished goods (like raw diamonds) that are incorporated into a finished product (cut and polished diamonds) and then re-exported. Complications arise when exported goods use raw materials and components some of which are imported and some produced domestically. The drawback in such cases means refund of an amount which represents the import duty paid on the imported materials used in the exported goods.

Duty-free Shop: A shop at airports, on ships etc. from where outgoing passengers may buy goods which are free of commodity taxes because the purchases are meant for exports. Similarly, incoming passengers may purchase certain goods from duty-free shop at a cheaper price than usual because they do not have to pay duty that is usually paid when goods are brought into a country.

Duty-free Zone: An area where goods may be unloaded, stored, and reshipped without payment of customs duty.

Ee

Earning Per Share: It means profit over a given period, reduced by preference dividend, divided by the number of shares outstanding at the end of that period.

Earning to Price Ratio: It is the ratio of the earning per share of a company to the market price of one share of that company.

E-banking: See Electronic Banking, *69*.

Electronic Banking (E-banking): It is a generic term encompassing internet banking, telephone banking, mobile banking etc. In other words, it is a process of delivery of banking services and products through electronic channels such as telephone, internet, cell phone etc. The concept and scope of E-banking is still evolving.

Electronic Cheque Conversion: Electronic cheque conversion is a process in which your cheque is used as a source of information—for the cheque number, your account number, and the number that identifies your financial institution. The information is then used to make a one-time electronic payment from your account—an electronic fund transfer. The cheque itself is not the method of payment.

Electronic Funds Transfer (EFT): The transfer of money between accounts by consumer electronic systems—such as automated teller machines (ATMs) and electronic payment of bills—rather than by cheque or cash.

Electronic Money (E-Money): In recent years, there has been a gradual switchover from the use of paper-based payments media to those based on electronics. While the basic characteristics of these new instruments are by and large similar to those of paper-based instruments, the former present a different set of challenges to policy makers. E-money is one such new product which has appeared on Indian horizon recently.

Definition and Kinds of E-money: E-money may be broadly defined as an electronic store of monetary value on a technical device used for making payments to undertakings other than the issuer without necessarily involving bank accounts in the transaction, but acting as a prepaid bearer instrument. E-money can be classified into the following two broad categories:

1. Pre-paid stored value card (also called electronic purse).
2. Pre-paid software-based product that uses computer networks such as internet (also referred to as digital cash or network money).

The stored value card scheme typically uses a microprocessor chip embedded in a plastic card while software based scheme typically uses specialised software installed in a personal computer. The stored value card could be of three types:

1. Single-purpose card.
2. Closed-system or limited-purpose card.
3. General-purpose or multi-purpose card.

The single-purpose card generally with a magnetic chip recording the amount of fund therein is designed to facilitate only one type of transaction, e.g. telephone calls, public transportation, laundry, parking facilities etc. In this case the distinguishing point is that the issuer and the service provider (acceptor) are identical for the cards. These cards are expected to substitute coins and currency notes.

Closed-system or limited-purpose card is generally used in a small number of well-identified points of sale within a well-identified location such as corporate/university campus.

Multi-purpose card can perform a variety of functions with several vendors, viz. credit card, debit card, stored value card, identification card, repository of personal medical information etc. The importance of these cards is especially underscored with respect to regulatory oversight, restrictions on issuers and their implications for monetary policy. These cards may reduce demand for current accounts in the bank for likely reduction in transaction costs, and prudent portfolio management.

It is important to distinguish here the so-called *access* products, e.g. credit card and debit card from e-money. The former typically require a telephone or a personal computer with appropriate software to access the customer account before transferring the value while under e-money, the amount of value is already embedded and it may be increased or reduced without necessarily involving a personal bank account. In a sense, e-money can be construed as an electronic form of traveller's cheques (TCs). In both cases, the user pays for the instrument upfront.

Benefits of E-money: Use and spread of e-money depends upon the incentives of issuers, merchants and consumers. For issuers, the principal motivation arises from revenues to be earned from investment of outstanding balances (i.e. float income), savings of costs from reduced handling of cash and incentive of offering fee-based service to consumers and merchants besides the larger security emanating from audit trail of transactions and improved management information system.

For merchants, the trade-off would be between reduction in cost of handling physical cash vis-à-vis cost of putting in place necessary infrastructure.

For consumers, the use of e-money would depend upon the perceived security and privacy of e-money and ease with which e-money could be used which would again depend upon willingness of merchants to accept e-money. In other words, apart from security, privacy and ease, network effects are also important for wider use of e-money.

An economy like India, where cash transactions are very high, could benefit from using e-money through cost savings from printing and minting of smaller denomination notes and coins and eliminating the cost of handling, storing, transporting and insuring currency. These should also improve operational efficiency of the financial sector as also extension of banking to the urban poor and rural communities besides facilitating e-governance initiatives of governments. However, such benefits should be weighed against the need to build up the costly infrastructure to operate nationwide cashless retail payment system.

Implications of E-money for the Central Bank: Before analysing the likely implications, it is instructive to note that e-money can be issued in three alternate ways. Each of these three ways may have different implications for conduct of monetary policy.

1. E-money can be issued in exchange of cash (i.e. 100 percent backing of central bank money). Under that circumstance, there may be only marginal change in total money supply in the economy provided there is no significant change in velocity of circulation of money.
2. E-money can also be issued on credit against interest payment.
3. E-money could also be issued as a separate form of currency independent of central bank money by entities other than the central bank. In that case, e-money would compete against the central bank money as a medium of exchange. However, such a scenario in which public gets e-money from an entity in exchange for something other than the central bank money seems remote now.

Currency notes and coins generally form an overwhelming part of the balance sheet of any central bank. If e-money is extensively used and in the process, replaces substantially central bank's money, central bank's balance sheet would *shrink* while that of the issuing authority of e-money would *expand* in relative terms.

With large scale use of e-money, it is apprehended that central bank's balance sheet may shrink to such an extent relative to that of the banking sector that it may be unable to perform its liquidity absorption function [in effect, open market operations (OMO)] on account of non-availability of adequate volume of assets. Under that circumstance, extensive e-monetisation in the economy could jeopardise the conduct of monetary policy of the central bank. It may, however, be noted that the central bank would not have any problem in liquidity injection because central bank money is still the only legal tender in the economy.

Apart from constraining its liquidity management function, relative shrinkage in balance sheet may also have implications regarding loss of *seigniorage* revenue for the central bank. This is because currency notes and coins are the interest-free liability of the central bank towards public (i.e. public have in effect lent to the central bank such amount free of interest) which are then used by the central bank to purchase interest bearing assets. Thus, interest earned on these assets constitutes its seigniorage revenue. Therefore, if the central bank's operating costs are high which are more likely in an environment where central bank is required to intervene more, it may even incur losses on account of seigniorage revenue foregone. This may also have adverse implications for governments with chronic budget deficits as they would be deprived of the transfer of surplus to its treasury from the profitable central bank.

A distinguishing characteristic of e-money is that unlike innovations in other retail payments media—which facilitate more efficient access to traditional form of central bank money—e-money could have the potential to become an independent medium of exchange. In that eventuality, two extreme views are being offered. On the one hand, one group perceives that in a highly technologically-advanced networked world, private entities may not require central bank money for settlement and, therefore, there may not be any central bank in future. Some of them also question whether private money is more efficient than central bank money from social welfare viewpoint and if so under what circumstance private money can replace central bank money altogether. On the other hand, there is another group of academicians and practitioners who strongly believe that central banks would continue to be as effective as ever though they may be required to respond differently in the changed environment.

E-Money in India: In India, where cash transactions are high in number, the use of e-money can be beneficial in terms of reduced miscellaneous costs, viz. cost of printing and minting of smaller denomination notes and coins and transportation and storage costs. However, certain additional costs for setting up of network infrastructure to operate nationwide are also associated with it. The RBI has been partnering a multi-application smart card project, under the aegis of the Ministry of Communications and Information Technology, Government of India, to run a pilot project on the use of multi-application smart cards in the country. Various issues relating to technology, security, regulatory and supervisory concerns and legal implications have been examined to make the use of smart cards a viable proposition after the conclusion of the pilot project. The project is aimed at combining applications relating to banking, insurance, postal services, identification, etc in a single card.

The Reserve Bank of India had constituted a Working Group on Electronic Money (Chairman: Zaire J. Camas) in January 2002 which submitted its Report in July 2002. The Group identified certain areas of concern from the point of view of the central bank in the context of more widespread use of e-money. Some of the suggestions made by the Group included: (a) multi-purpose e-money to be issued only by authorised banks on a credit basis which should be strictly regulated and closely monitored, (b) redeemability should be ensured in order to preserve the unit of account function of money as well as to control money supply in the economy, and (c) reporting of e-money statistics should be ensured for the purposes of monetary policy and protection against criminal abuse such as money laundering. See also Money.

Embargo: It is an official order that restricts/forbids trade, movement of ships etc with other country/countries.

Embezzlement: Embezzlement is defined as theft/larceny of assets (money or property) by a person in a position of trust or responsibility over those assets. Embezzlement typically occurs in the employment and corporate settings.

E-money: See Electronic Money, *69*.

Encoding: The process used to imprint or inscribe MICR (Magnetic Ink Character Recognition) characters on cheques, deposits, and other financial instruments. MICR is a character-recognition technology adopted mainly by the banking industry to facilitate the processing of cheques.

Error Resolution: The required process for resolving errors involving electronic transfers to and from deposit accounts.

Escheat: Reversion of real or personal property to the state when: (a) a person dies without leaving a will and has no heirs, or (b) when the property (such as a bank account) has been inactive for a certain period of time.

Escrow: A financial instrument held by a third party on behalf of the other two parties in a transaction. The funds are held by the escrow service until it receives the appropriate written or oral instructions—or until obligations have been fulfilled. Securities, funds, and other assets can be held in escrow.

Escrow Account: An escrow account is a special bank account into which earnings from sales (e.g. convertible currency proceeds from exports) are accumulated. These revenues are set aside for subsequent acquisition of goods and services from a foreign supplier. The escrowed money, usually interest-bearing, is disbursed by the bank to the foreign supplier under payment terms and against documents specified in the supplier's sale contract.

Escrow Analysis: The periodic examination of escrow accounts by a mortgage company to verify that monthly deposits are sufficient to pay taxes, insurance, and other escrow-related items when due.

Escrow Funds: Funds held in reserve by a mortgage company to pay taxes, insurance, and other mortgage-related items when due.

Estate Account: An account held in the name of a decedent that is administered by an executor or administrator of the estate.

Estate Duty: It is a levy on the value of the entire estate left behind by a decedent before its division among the inheritors. It is contrasted with an Inheritance Tax (q.v.) which is based on the share of the estate received by each beneficiary. Estate duty (or death duty) is simpler and more productive than inheritance tax because the former avoids the difficult task of determining the value of the share of each inheritor. Estate duty is usually levied at a progressive rate to reduce economic disparities.

Euro: This is the name of a new common currency of the 18 (out of 28) European Union member countries which replaced all other currencies of the member countries. It was introduced on January 1, 1999 and became fully operational by January 2002. Euro's birth was hailed as a historic turning point in international finance and was arguably the greatest single step in the drive to create a united Europe from the ruins of Second World War.

The euro zone grouping (Austria, Belgium, Cyprus, Estonia, Finland, France, Germany, Greece, Ireland, Italy, Latvia, Luxembourg, Malta, Netherlands, Portugal, Slovakia, Slovenia and Spain) accounts for nearly a fifth of world economic output and trade. The following 10 countries, though EU Members States, are not currently participating in the single currency: Britain, Croatia, Denmark, Sweden, Bulgaria, Czech Republic, Lithuania, Hungary, Poland and Romania.

Economic and monetary union has been a recurring ambition of the European Union since the late 1960s because it promises both currency stability and a strong advance towards the integration of Europe. The transition to euro was smooth because the changeover was backed by solid legal guarantees and the financial markets were carefully preparing for the creation of the euro. Stability of euro is guaranteed by the fact that conditions laid down for its creation are strict and that it will be managed by an independent central bank. See also European Union.

List of 18 Members States of the European Union Participating in the Single Currency Euro (as on 30.04.2014)

Austria	Euro (Schillings)
Belgium	Euro (Franc)
Cyprus	Euro (Pound)
Estonia	Euro (Kroon)
Finland	Euro (Markkaa)
France	Euro (Franc)
Germany	Euro (Deutsche Mark)
Greece	Euro (Drachma)
Ireland	Euro (Pound)
Italy	Euro (Lira)
Latvia	Euro (Lats)
Luxembourg	Euro (Franc)
Malta	Euro (Lira)
Netherlands	Euro (Guilder)
Portugal	Euro (Escudo)
Slovakia	Euro (Slovak Koruna)
Slovenia	Euro (Tolar)
Spain	Euro (Peseta)

Note: Expressions in parentheses indicate name of the money unit prior to switchover to Euro.

Eurobanks: These are banks dealing in Eurocurrency/Eurodollar deposits or issuance of Eurobonds.

Eurodollar: It refers to dollar deposits owned by someone other than a resident of US. The concept of Eurodollar came into existence in Europe during the late 1950s with the advent of currency convertibility. At that time, US was losing dollars due to balance of payments deficit. These dollars were being deposited in European banks. Since dollar is the most acceptable currency, it moves from one country to another in search of higher interest rates. This movement of dollars has limited the effect of an independent monetary policy. For example, a country facing inflation may raise interest rate. However, this hike can attract more dollars leading to higher domestic money supply.

European Union (EU): A 28-nation economic union in Western Europe comprising of Austria, Belgium, Croatia, Cyprus, Estonia, Finland, France, Germany, Greece, Ireland, Italy, Latvia, Luxembourg, Malta, Netherlands, Portugal, Slovakia, Slovenia, Spain, Britain, Denmark, Sweden, Bulgaria, Czech Republic, Lithuania, Hungary, Poland, and Romania.

EU is the concrete expression of the common desire of the sovereign nations of Europe to work and live together. As an advanced form of multi-sectoral integration, its competence extends to the economy, industry, politics, and citizens' rights of the Member States. The EU is India's largest trading partner, accounting for about one-third of both India's exports and imports. However, India's share in the EU's imports and exports is less than 1 percent. See also Euro.

Ex: In finance, ex means *without, not including.* In commerce, ex means *from*. Thus, ex warehouse means *sold from a warehouse, i.e.* buyer of the goods has to provide and pay for transport from the warehouse. Similarly, ex factory price means price from or at the factory, i.e. price before the inclusion of excise duty. Ex as a prefix means former, e.g. ex prime minister.

Exchange Control: It means control on the purchase and sale of foreign exchange at the official exchange rate by the central bank of a country. Regulation of foreign exchange transactions is generally done by a country facing balance of payments deficit in order to keep the foreign exchange reserves at appropriate level.

Exchange Rate: It is the rate at which the currency of one country is converted into another currency. For example, ₹ 61 = 1 US$ is Indian rupee exchange rate for one US dollar.

Exchange Rationing: In the face of excess demand for foreign exchange over available supplies, the need is felt for its judicious allocation among individuals and firms which have to make payments for imports. Rationing is done according to the intensity and urgency of the need. It may also be used to force bilateral trade balancing, i.e. more is kept for imports from country A with which the country concerned has trade relations than for country B with which trade is not much.

Excise Duty: It is a tax on goods produced or manufactured within a country. It is collected from the producers of excisable goods. Excise duty is levied either on *ad valorem* basis (i.e. as a percentage of the value of production) or on specific basis (i.e. as a stated amount per unit of weight, volume etc.) or on *ad valorem*-cum-specific basis.

Exclusions: See Exemptions, *79*.

Exemptions: Exemptions (or exclusions) are those items which are explicitly and statutorily freed from the scope of a tax and therefore remain untaxed. They may be termed as non-taxable gross receipts. Several considerations weigh on a government to declare a host of receipts exempt, either fully or up to specified limits, from the scope of taxation.

Income tax laws of most countries describe incomes that are exempt from the purview of income tax, i.e. tax-free incomes. These exemptions serve various socio-economic objectives through the medium of tax policy. In developing countries, agricultural incomes are generally exempt from income tax owing to administrative difficulties of reaching out to widely dispersed small and marginal farmers who in most cases are illiterate. Incomes of charitable and religious trusts are generally exempt from taxes. However, if the number of exemptions is very large, it will narrow the tax base besides making the law complex. See also Tax Holiday.

EXIM Bank: See Export Import Bank of India, *80*.

Expense Account: It refers to allocation of money which a businessman is allowed to spend personally on travelling and entertaining clients in connection with his business.

Export Duty: See Customs Duty, *56*.

Export Import Bank of India (EXIM Bank): It was established in January 1982, to which the export finance functions of the IDBI were transferred. The EXIM Bank was also made eligible to loans and advances from the National Industrial Credit (Long-Term Operations) Fund operated by the RBI.

Exports: Goods and services that are produced domestically and sold to buyers in another country.

External Commercial Borrowings (ECBs): ECBs provide an additional source of funds for corporates to finance the expansion of existing capacity as well as new investment, taking cognisance of interest rate differentials between domestic and international markets and the associated market risks. ECBs include commercial bank loans, buyers' credit, suppliers' credit, securitised instruments such as Floating Rate Notes and Fixed Rate Bonds and, commercial borrowings from the private sector window of multilateral financial institutions such as International Financial Corporation (IFC) and Asian Development Bank (ADB). An important objective of ECB policy in India has been to provide flexibility in borrowings by Indian corporates, while maintaining prudent limits for total external borrowings.

Ff

Face Value: Face value (or par value or nominal value) is the value printed on a document such as a share certificate. The printed value need not represent the issue price, redemption price or current market price.

Faked Invoicing: In order to take advantage of export subsidies, import entitlements etc., there is a tendency for over-invoicing of exports so that higher premiums can be earned. When these incentives are withdrawn, over-invoicing becomes less attractive and so exports are also shown to be less. Similarly, if imports are on restricted category, there is a tendency to under-invoice them so that more volume of them could be had.

FDI: See Foreign Direct Investment, *97*.

Federal Reserve System (FRS): It is the principal monetary authority (central bank) of the US which issues currency and regulates the supply of credit in the economy. It consists of 12 regional FRS banks in the US which carry out the role of a central bank. The twelve banks are in Boston, New York, Philadelphia, Cleveland, Richmond, Atlanta, Chicago, St. Louis, Minneapolis, Kansas City, Dallas and San Francisco.

Fiat Money: See Money, *155*.

Fiduciary: Undertaking to act as executor, administrator, guardian, conservator, or trustee for a family trust, authorized trust, or testamentary trust, or receiver or trustee in bankruptcy.

Fiduciary Money: See Money, *155*.

Financial Asset: It is a financial claim on the rest of the world represented by a contractual obligation (such as a loan) or evidenced by a security (such as a share certificate). Monetary gold is treated as a financial asset because it is readily available for payment of international obligations.

Financial Derivatives: In recent years, complex financial products such as asset-backed securities, derivatives, credit-default swaps (CDSs) and collateralised debt obligations (CDOs) have proliferated in developed countries. These products have become highly popular with banks and financial institutions as they allow them to hedge their risks and manage their regulatory and economic capital more efficiently.

The emergence of the market for derivative products, most notably forwards, futures and options, can be traced back to the willingness of risk-averse economic agents to guard themselves against uncertainties arising out of fluctuations in asset prices. By their very nature, the financial markets are marked by a very high degree of volatility. Through the use of derivative products, it is possible to partially or fully transfer price risks by locking-in asset prices. As instruments of risk management, derivatives generally do not influence the fluctuations in the underlying asset prices. However, by locking-in asset prices, derivative products minimize the impact of fluctuations in asset prices on the profitability and cash flow situation of risk-averse investors.

Derivative products initially emerged as hedging devices against fluctuations in commodity prices and commodity-linked derivatives remained the sole form of such products for a long time. The financial derivatives came into spotlight in post-1970 period due to growing instability in the financial markets. However, since their emergence, financial derivatives have become very popular. In recent years, the market for financial derivatives has grown tremendously both in terms of variety of instruments available, their complexity and also turnover.

In India also financial products such as mortgage-backed securities (MBS) and asset-backed securities (ABS) are in existence. Besides the securitised products, the Indian forex and rupee derivative markets have also developed significantly over the years.

In respect of forex derivatives involving rupee, residents have access to foreign exchange forward contracts, foreign currency-rupee swap instruments and currency options—both cross currency and foreign currency-rupee. As stated in the Annual Policy Statement for the year 2008-09, the Reserve Bank of India (RBI) announced the introduction of currency futures in the eligible exchanges for which the broad framework was announced in August 2008. In future, some more innovative and complex products might emerge. These products may pose several regulatory and supervisory challenges.

Meaning of Derivatives: Derivative in mathematics means a variable derived from another variable. The term *derivative* indicates that it has no independent value, i.e. its value is entirely *derived* from the value of the underlying asset. The underlying asset can be security, commodity, bullion, currency, live stock or anything else. In other words, derivative means a forward, future, option or any other hybrid contract of pre-determined fixed duration, linked for the purpose of contract fulfilment to the value of a specified real or financial asset of an index of securities. Similarly, in the financial sense, a derivative is a financial product, which has been derived from a market for another product. Without the underlying product, derivatives do not have any independent existence in the market.

Derivative instruments are defined by the Indian Securities Contracts (Regulation) Act, 1956 to include: (i) a security derived from a debt instrument, share, secured/unsecured loan, risk instrument or contract for differences, or any other form of security, and (ii) a contract that derives its value from the prices/index of prices of underlying securities.

In other words, derivatives are financial instruments/contracts whose value depends upon the value of an underlying. Since their value is essentially derived out of an underlying, they are financial abstractions whose value is derived mathematically from the changes in the value of the underlying.

The International Monetary Fund (IMF) defines derivatives as "financial instruments that are linked to a specific financial instrument or indicator or commodity and through which specific financial risks can be traded in financial markets in their own right. The value of a financial derivative derives from the price of an underlying item, such as an asset or index. Unlike debt securities, no principal is advanced to be repaid and no investment income accrues".

Derivatives have come into being because of the existence of risks in business. Thus, derivatives are means of managing risks. The parties managing risks in the market are known as *hedgers*. Some people/organizations are in the business of taking risks to earn profits. Such entities represent the *speculators*. The third players in the market, known as the *arbitragers,* take advantage of the market mistakes.

In recent years, derivatives have become increasingly important in the field of finance. While futures and options are now actively traded on many exchanges, forward contracts are popular on the over-the-counter (OTC) market.

Variants (or Types) of Derivative Contracts: Derivative contracts have several variants. The most common variants are forwards, futures, options and swaps.

Forwards/Forward Contracts: A forward contract is a customised contract between two entities, where settlement takes place on a specific date in the future at today's pre-agreed price. A forward contract is an agreement to buy or sell an asset on a specified date for specified price. One of the parties to the contract assumes a long position and agrees to buy the underlying asset on a certain specified future date, for a certain specified price. The other party assumes a short position and agrees to sell the asset on the same date for the same price. Other contract details like delivery date, price and quantity are negotiated bilaterally by the parties to the contract. See also full entry on Forwards/Forward Contracts.

Futures/Future Contracts: Future contracts are special types of forward contracts in the sense that the former are standardised exchange-traded contracts. Future contract markets are designed to solve the problems that exist in forward markets. A future contract is an agreement between two parties to buy or sell an asset at a certain time in future, at a certain price. However, unlike forward contracts, future contracts are standardized and stock exchange-traded. To facilitate liquidity in the future contracts, the exchange specifies certain standard features for the contract. It is a standardized contract with a standard underlying instrument, a standard quantity and quality of the underlying instrument that can be delivered, and a standard timing of such settlement. See also full entry on Futures/Future Contracts.

Options: Options are fundamentally different from forward and future contracts. An option gives the holder of the option the right to do something. The holder does not have to necessarily exercise this right. In contrast, in a forward or future contract, the two parties commit themselves to doing something. Whereas it costs nothing (except margin requirements) to enter into a future contract, the purchase of an option requires an up front payment.

Options are of two types: calls options and put options. Calls options give the buyer the right but not the obligation to buy a given quantity of the underlying asset, at a given price on or before a given future date. Put options give the buyer the right, but not the obligation to sell a given quantity of the underlying asset at a given price on or before a given date. See also full entry on Options.

Swaps: Swaps are private agreements between two parties to exchange cash flows in the future according to a pre-arranged formula. They can be regarded as portfolios of forward contracts. Following are the two commonly used swaps:

- **Interest Rate Swaps:** These entail swapping of only the interest-related cash flows between the parties in the same currency.
- **Currency Swaps:** These entail swapping of both principal and interest between the parties, with the cash flows in one direction being in a different currency than those in the opposite direction.

Swaptions: Swaptions are options to buy or sell a swap that will become operative at the expiry of the options. Thus, swaption is an option on a forward swap. Rather than have call options and put options, the swaptions market has receiver swaptions and payer swaptions.

Financial Exclusion and Financial Inclusion: In most developing countries, a large segment of society, particularly low-income people, has very little access to financial services, both formal and semi-formal. As a consequence, many of them have to necessarily depend either on their own or high cost informal sources of finance such as moneylenders. This is particularly true for the sporadic financing requirements of low income households for non-productive consumption purposes and other emergency requirements such as medical expenditure. Benefits of growth, therefore, tend to concentrate in the hands of those already served by the formal financial system.

Despite the rapid spread of banking over the years, a significant segment of the population, predominantly in the rural areas, is excluded from the formal financial system. It is well-known that poor people, potential entrepreneurs, small enterprises and others are excluded from the financial sector, which leads to their marginalisation and denial of opportunity for them to grow and prosper. Therefore, access to a greater proportion of the population to the organised financial system should be high on the agenda of the Government of India. The key issue, however, is how to mainstream the institutional sources so as to achieve wider coverage in terms of extending credit. There are also a large number of households with low income and small savings, which need to be mobilised.

Apart from the rural areas, there is significant degree of financial exclusion in urban areas as well. The cost of financial exclusion is recognised to be enormous for the society as well as for individuals, particularly in terms of inability to realise full potential due to financial constraints.

The recent developments in banking technology have transformed banking from the traditional brick-and-mortar infrastructure like staffed branches to a system supplemented by other channels like automated teller machines (ATMs), credit/debit cards, internet banking, online money transfers etc. However, the access to such technology is restricted only to certain segments of the society. Indeed, trends such as increasingly sophisticated customer segmentation technology—allowing, for example, more accurate targeting of sections of the market—have led to restricted access to financial services for some groups. There is a growing divide, with an increased range of personal finance options for a segment of high and upper middle income population and a significantly large section of the population who lack access to even the most basic banking services. This is termed *financial exclusion*. These people, particularly, those living on low incomes, cannot access mainstream financial products such as bank accounts, remittance and payment services, financial advisory services, etc.

Merely having a bank account may not be a good indicator of financial inclusion. The ideal definition should look at people who want to access financial services but are denied the same. If genuine claimants for credit and financial services are denied the same, then that is a case of exclusion. As this aspect would raise the issue of credit worthiness or bankability, it is also necessary to dwell upon what could be done to make the claimants of institutional credit bankable or creditworthy. This would require re-engineering of existing financial products or delivery systems and making them more in tune with the expectations and absorptive capacity of the intended clientele.

According to the Committee on Financial Inclusion (Chairman: C. Rangarajan), 2008, "Financial inclusion may be defined as the process of ensuring access to financial services and timely and adequate credit where needed by vulnerable groups such as weaker sections and low income groups at an affordable cost."

The essence of financial inclusion is in trying to ensure that a range of appropriate financial services is available to every individual and enabling them to understand and access those services. Apart from the regular form of financial intermediation, it may include a basic no-frills banking account for making and receiving payments, a savings product suited to the pattern of cash flows of a poor household, money transfer facilities, small loans and overdrafts for productive, personal and other purposes, insurance (life and non-life) etc. While financial inclusion, in the narrow sense, may be achieved to some extent by offering any one of these services, the objective of *comprehensive financial inclusion* would be to provide a holistic set of services encompassing all of the above.

Advantages of Financial Inclusion: Access to safe, easy and affordable credit and other financial services by the poor and vulnerable groups, disadvantaged areas and lagging sectors is recognised as a pre-condition for accelerating growth and reducing income disparities and poverty. A developing country can benefit from financial inclusion in the following ways:

1. Access to a well-functioning financial system—by creating equal opportunities—enables economically and socially excluded people to integrate effectively into the economy and contribute to development and protect themselves against economic shocks.
2. Financial inclusion enables to finance activities or firms or individuals that are at the margin, thereby promoting their growth-inducing productive activities.
3. Availability of external finance to potential entrepreneurs and small firms enables new entrants, leading to increased competition to incumbents. This, in turn, encourages entrepreneurship and productivity.
4. Inclusive finance—including safe savings, appropriately designed loans for poor and low-income households and for micro, small and medium-sized enterprises, and appropriate insurance and payments services—can help people to enhance incomes, acquire capital, manage risk, and come out of poverty.
5. It has been well-recognised that access to financial services facilitates making and receiving financial payments and reduces transaction costs.

6. Access to financial services contributes to higher production and social protection, as the financial sector—through stored savings, credit and insurance—serves as a measure of crisis mitigation.

Strategy for Building an Inclusive Financial Sector: Bringing the larger population within the structured and organised financial system has to be an important item on the development agenda of a government. While several central banks focus solely on inflation, many in developed and emerging economies alike, including India, also focus on growth. The RBI has, therefore, introduced various new measures to encourage the expansion of financial coverage in the country. Financial inclusion is considered essential for fostering economic growth in a more inclusive fashion.

In a fast growing economy, an important issue is how to sustain and diversify growth so that the risk to growth process is diversified across sectors. It is in this context that the search for potential sources of incremental growth, i.e. sectors that have difficulty in accessing financial services, assumes importance. Therefore, including such segments or sectors would, on the one hand, unleash their productive capacities, and on the other, would augment domestic demand on a sustainable basis driven by income and consumption growth from such sectors. This would also have strong inter-sectoral linkages.

Overall strategy for building an inclusive financial sector may be based on:

1. Effecting improvements within the existing formal credit delivery mechanism;
2. Measures for improving credit absorption capacity especially amongst marginal and sub marginal farmers and poor non-cultivator households;
3. Evolving new models for effective outreach; and
4. Leveraging on technology based solutions.

Recent Measures for Financial Inclusion: Given the socio-demographic complexities in India, the policy endeavour of the RBI has been to adopt a multi-institutional and multi-instrument approach to comprehensively address the issue of financial inclusion in all its dimensions, going beyond mere availability of credit to the masses. The term *financial inclusion* needs to be understood in a broader perspective to mean the provision of the full range of affordable financial services, viz. access to payments and remittance facilities, savings, loans and insurance services by the formal financial system to those who tend to be excluded from these services. The RBI, while recognising the concerns in regard to the banking practices that tend to exclude rather than attract vast sections of population, has been urging the banks to review their existing practices to align them with the objective of achieving greater financial inclusion. The RBI too has taken a number of measures with the objective of attracting the financially excluded population into the formalised financial system. Some of the measures taken in this direction are as follows:

No Frills Account: With a view to achieving greater financial inclusion, banks were advised in November 2005 to make available a basic banking *no frills account* either with 'nil' or very low minimum balances as well as charges that would make such accounts accessible to vast sections of population. All the public and the private sector banks as well as the foreign banks, except those not having significant retail presence, are reported to have introduced the basic banking 'no-frills' account.

***General Credit Card (GCC)*:** With the objective of providing hassle-free credit to the banks' constituents in rural and semi urban areas, the banks were advised in December 2005, to consider introduction of a *General Credit Card* (GCC) to such constituents. The card was to have a credit limit of up to ₹ 25,000, based on the assessment of income and cash flows of the household without insistence on security or purpose or end-use of credit. The credit facility was to be in the nature of revolving credit entitling the holder to withdraw up to the limit sanctioned. The banks are required to charge appropriate and reasonable Interest rate on the facility.

***Business Facilitator and Business Correspondent (BC) Models*:** In January 2006, banks were permitted to utilise the services of non-governmental organisations (NGOs/SHGs), micro-finance institutions and other civil society organisations as intermediaries in providing financial and banking services through the use of *business facilitator and business correspondent (BC) models*. The BC model allows banks to do *cash in-cash out* transactions at the location of the BC and allows branchless banking.

Passbook Facility: The matter of issuing passbooks to the small depositors has been a nagging issue for sometime past. Pass books provide the account holders a ready reckoner of the transactions in their accounts and is a convenient reference document—which can not be substituted by periodical bank account statements, particularly by the small account holders. Since non-issuance of the pass books to the small customers could indirectly lead to their financial exclusion, the RBI had advised the banks in October 2006 to invariably offer the pass book facility to all its savings bank account holders (individuals) and not to levy any charge on the customers thereof.

Simplified KYC Procedure: With a view to facilitating the opening of bank accounts by the common man through a simplified KYC procedure, in the Mid-Term Review of the Annual Policy of the RBI for the year 2006-07, it was announced that the "banks could open accounts of low balance/turnover (where the balance does not exceed ₹ 50,000 in all the accounts taken together and the total credit in all the accounts taken together is not expected to exceed ₹ 2 lakh in a year) only with self certification of address by the customers and his photograph". However, this policy announcement is yet to be operationalised as the matter is under consideration of the Government in the light of the provisions of the Rules framed under Prevention of Money Laundering Act.

Credit Counselling and Financial Education: Promoting *credit counselling and financial education* of the clientele of the banks is also an area that deserves due attention of the banking community. Towards this objective, the banks were also advised by the RBI to make available all printed material used by retail customers in the concerned regional language. As far as RBI itself is concerned, it has launched on June 18, 2007, a multilingual website in 13 Indian languages on all matters concerning banking and the common person so that the language does not become a barrier to acquiring financial education by the public at large.

Financial Inclusion: See Financial Exclusion and Financial Inclusion, *86*.

Financial Infrastructure: It means presence of well-established institutions, soundness of bank balance sheets, existence of adequate safety nets and vigilant supervision of the financial system of a country.

Financial Intermediaries: Financial intermediaries are an integral part of a modern industrial economy. They are institutions which act as middlemen between the lenders and the borrowers. They specialise in the purchase and sale of financial assets. More specifically, they buy primary securities and sell secondary securities. Financial intermediaries are classified into two main categories: (a) banks, and (b) non-banking financial institutions like Unit Trust of India (q.v.). Financial intermediaries are beneficial both to lenders and borrowers. Lenders stand to gain because they can invest their funds at low risk and greater liquidity with financial institutions. The main advantage to borrowers is availability of adequate credit at reasonable rate of interest.

How are financial intermediaries able to benefit both lenders and borrowers and also to make profit for themselves in the process? The secret of their economic success lies in the economies of scale in asset management. They diversify their asset holdings in such a manner as to strike an optimum balance between security and profitability. For this purpose, the financial institutions employ professional managers and financial analysts who evaluate investment opportunities and take appropriate decisions. Because of the large volume of business, the establishment cost per unit of transaction is lower as compared to that of an individual investor.

Financial Market: It is a market in which financial assets of various kinds like shares, debentures and bills are dealt with. A financial market consists of: (a) money market which deals in short-term credit, and (b) capital market which provides medium-term and long-term credit.

In a developing country like India money market is sub-divided into: (a) organised market, and (b) unorganised market. Commercial banks, co-operative banks and non-banking financial institutions comprise the organised sector of the money market. This market operates under the control, guidance and supervision of the central bank. The unorganised money market predominates in rural areas and is composed of indigenous bankers and moneylenders. It is generally free from the monetary and credit controls of the central bank. It operates without a set of well-defined rules and regulations and is, therefore, exploitative in its dealings. The malpractices of moneylenders are well-known.

Like money market, the capital market is also divided into two sectors: (a) organised market comprising of development banks, share market and mutual funds, and (b) unorganised market consisting of hire purchase companies, chit funds, finance companies etc. The unorganised sector of the capital market has limited importance.

Financial Openness: It means opening up of the financial sector in terms of entry of foreign entities and easing of restrictions on international transactions.

Financial Regulatory Agency: An organization authorized by statute for ensuring the safe and sound operation of financial institutions chartered to conduct business under that agency's jurisdiction.

Financial Repression: It is a term meaning excessive government controls on financial system of a country. It includes: (a) high required reserve ratios, (b) subsidised or directed credit programmes, (c) credit rationing, (d) ceilings on deposit, and (e) fixing maximum interest rates on loans.

Financial System: It refers to the whole gamut of institutional arrangements which help to mobilise financial surpluses of an economy and transfer them to areas of financial deficit. Financial system of a country rests on three pillars: (a) financial institutions or financial intermediaries, (b) financial markets, and (c) financial assets. Financial system is the linchpin of a modern industrial economy. It promotes savings by providing a wide variety of financial assets to the general public. Savings collected from the household sector are pooled together and allocated to various sectors of the economy for raising production level. If the allocation of credit is socially equitable, it will help in reducing interregional inequalities.

Financial Year: It is the year of account for financial purposes, often not coinciding with the calendar year. For example, in India the financial year (or fiscal year) runs from April 1 to March 31 of the following year. In US, the fiscal year runs from July 1 to June 30.

First Mortgage: A real estate loan which is in a first lien position, taking priority over all other liens. In case of a foreclosure, the first mortgage will be repaid before any other mortgages.

Fiscal Policy: Fiscal policy is an important instrument of the general economic policy of a government. It is concerned with the use of a government's taxation and expenditure powers to influence economic activities in an economy at the aggregate level. It also deals with financial relations between different tiers of government in a federal polity. Through the medium of budget, fiscal policy determines the level of taxation, public expenditure, borrowings and the issue of additional currency by a government. See also Monetary Policy.

Fixed Asset: See Asset, *8*.

Floating Exchange Rate: It is a system in which the prices of various currencies relative to each other are set by the forces of demand and supply in the market without any intervention by the government.

Floating Insurance Policy: It gives the regular overseas trader insurance in advance for all his shipments for some period ahead; the length of the period depending on the shipments made from time to time under the policy and on the sum insured.

Foreclosure: A legal process in which property that is collateral or security for a loan may be sold to help repay the loan when the loan is in default.

Foreign Aid: Economists usually consider aid as international flow of resources in the form of public development assistance. If this assistance is from individual national governments, it is called *bilateral aid.* If it is from international donor agencies like UNO and other global bodies, regional development banks and aid consortia, it is called *multilateral aid.*

Thus, foreign aid is any international transfer made on concessional terms (rather than at market/commercial terms) for promoting economic development. International financial transfers can take two forms: (a) grants, and (b) loans. Grants are unilateral transfers which are not to be repaid. Loans carry relatively lower rate of interest and longer period of repayment. Foreign aid may take a variety of physical forms such as capital goods, commodities (especially food), technical assistance and military equipment. Normally, military aid is not considered as part of foreign aid.

Many believe that foreign aid from rich countries is indispensable for the development of less developed countries (LDCs). If LDCs wish to emerge from poverty, they must save and invest. Foreign aid can help them fill the gap between low level of domestic savings and desired level of investment. Foreign aid may bring with it managerial skills and technical know-how. This will help LDCs to discard their outdated methods of production. Better technology is the key to increased productivity. It is also argued that aid is an international redistributive mechanism. The widening gap between developed and underdeveloped countries can be reduced through foreign aid. It is the moral duty of the rich nations to help the starving people of Africa and Asia. The present poverty of LDCs is partly attributed to their economic exploitation by the developed countries of Europe and America.

Adverse repercussions of foreign aid are also noteworthy. Opponents believe that foreign aid is neither a necessary nor a sufficient condition for emerging from poverty. There is considerably more to development than just injections of aid. Economic achievement depends on people's own faculties, motivations, ways of life, institutions and the policies of their rulers.

Giving aid reinforces the fatalist attitudes of LDCs. It also creates feeling of inferiority among the people of recipient country. Aid impairs the spirit of competitiveness among LDCs. If aid is in the form of loans, it adds to the burden of debt which is already massive in amount in the case of LDCs. Repayment of loans leads to foreign exchange outflows from LDCs, accentuating their balance of payment difficulties.

Almost invariably, aid is available to LDCs with restrictions, particularly regarding its use. The tying of aid may take the following forms:

Source-tying or Procurement-tying: It specifies where the recipient can spend aid. The spending restrictions usually take the form of tying aid to purchases in the donor country. This reduces the real worth of aid because it prevents recipients from shopping around the world to find exactly the goods they want in the cheapest markets. The recipient country must buy imports in the donor country and they are to be transported in ships of donor country.

Use-tying: Aid is tied to specific projects which may not be in line with the development goals of LDCs.

Double-tying: More often than not, both restrictions operate together, leading to double tying. This has been extremely expensive for LDCs. The prices from tied sources are much higher than the international prices.

Aid-tying is justified by the donors as necessary for overcoming their balance of payment deficits. However, source-tying is adopted by not only balance of payment deficit countries but also by surplus countries.

Source-tying is also governed by the desire of donors to support their industries with excess capacity or to get rid of their surplus stocks of commodities. Thus, aid with strings is less useful for LDCs than it may appear overtly. In fact, tied-aid creates more jobs and leads to the establishment and expansion of more industries in the donor than in the donee country.

Foreign Direct Investment (FDI): Investment in one country by individuals and organisations from another is an important aspect of international economics. Investment may be for portfolio (i.e. in the form of securities) or direct capital (i.e. productive facilities).

According to the International Monetary Fund, FDI is defined as "investment that is made to acquire a lasting interest in an enterprise operating in an economy other than that of the investor. The investor's purpose being to have an effective voice in the management of the enterprise." The essence of FDI is the transmission to the host country of a package of capital, managerial, skill and technical knowledge.

As a matter of clarification, it is important to distinguish between FDI and portfolio investment. FDI is generally defined as a form of long-term international capital movement, made for the purpose of productive activity and accompanied by the intention of managerial control or participation in the management of a foreign firm. FDI should not be confused with portfolio investment which does not seek management control, but is motivated by profit. Portfolio investment occurs when individual investors invest, mostly through stockbrokers, in stocks of foreign companies in foreign land in search of profit opportunities.

Global private investment, in most part, is now made by transnational corporations (TNCs) also referred to as multinational corporations (MNCs). Clearly, these transnational organisations play a major role in world trade and investments because of their demonstrated management skills, technology, financial resources, and related advantages.

Dilemma is faced by developing nations in formulating policies covering investments by foreigners. They usually have an urgent need for foreign investment assistance, but domestic political considerations often dictate severe tax and other laws, including nationalisation laws, which discourage new foreign investment. Many developing nations have been successful, however, in providing attractive tax and other incentives to foreign investors for sufficient time periods to ensure a satisfactory return on the original investment.

Advantages: Private foreign investment, mostly by multinational corporations, is an important form of international flow of financial resources. Foreign investment takes place for private gain but it has the following potential benefits for less developed countries (LDCs):

1. Foreign investment can fill the gap between desired investment and locally mobilised savings.
2. It can fill the gap between desired foreign exchange requirements and those derived from net export earnings.
3. Foreign investment can supply a package of needed resources such as management experience, entrepreneurial abilities, organisational and technological skills.
4. Foreign investment brings with it technological knowledge while transferring machinery and equipment to LDCs.
5. Foreign investment can create employment in the modern sectors of LDCs.
6. It can benefit consumers in LDCs through lower prices/improved quality of goods and through new products.

7. Foreign investment can stimulate domestic investment through forward and backward linkages. For example, output of a foreign firm can be an input of domestic industries. Similarly, output of the domestic industries can be inputs for the foreign firms. If this is so, foreign firms create demand for industries producing goods purchased by them.

Disadvantages: Foreign private investment is not an unmixed blessing. Governments of LDCs have to be very careful while deciding the magnitude, pattern and conditions of private foreign investment. The adverse implications of foreign investment are the following:

1. When foreign investment is competitive with home investment, the profits in domestic industries fall, leading to fall in domestic savings.
2. Contribution of foreign firms to public revenue through corporate taxes is considerably less because of liberal tax concessions, excessive investment allowances, disguised public subsidies and tariff protection provided by the host government.
3. Foreign firms reinforce dualistic socio-economic structure and increase income inequalities. They create a small number of highly paid modern sector executives. They divert resources away from priority sectors to the manufacture of sophisticated products for the consumption of local elites. As they are located in urban areas, they create imbalance between rural and urban opportunities, accelerating flow of rural population to urban areas.
4. Foreign firms stimulate inappropriate consumption patterns through excessive advertising and monopolistic/oligopolistic market power. The products made by multinationals for the domestic markets behind tariff walls are not necessarily low in price and high in quality. Their technology is generally capital-intensive which does not suit the needs of a labour-surplus economy.
5. Foreign firms are able to extract sizeable economic and political concessions from competing governments of LDCs.

These concessions may take the form of excessive protection, tax rebates and investment allowances. Consequently, private profits of these companies may exceed social bencfits.

6. Foreign firms try to avoid local taxes by artificially inflating the price they pay for intermediate products purchased from overseas affiliates so as to lower their stated local profits. This is known as *transfer pricing* and host governments have no control over this. They can also avoid the effects of domestic monetary policy because of easy access to foreign capital markets and their internal resources.
7. Continual outflow of profits is too large in many cases, putting pressure on foreign exchange reserves. Foreign investors are very particular about profit repatriation facilities.
8. Foreign firms may influence political decisions in LDCs. In view of their large size and power, national sovereignty and control over economic policy may be jeopardised. In extreme cases, they (foreign firms) may bribe public officials at the highest levels. Similarly, they may contribute to *friendly* political parties and subvert the political process of the host country.

Determinants of FDI: To understand the scale and direction of FDI flows, it is necessary to identify their major determinants. Factors influencing the destination of investment, i.e. the host-country determinants are examined below.

Size of the Market: Large countries provide substantial markets where the consumer demand for certain goods has been largely unfilled to date. This potential has been a draw for many of the initial foreign-owned operations in these countries. This explains the massive FDI flows which the large size of China's market has attracted since early 1980s. In many cases, the establishment of a low cost marketing operation represents the first step by a multinational into the market of the country. This establishes a presence in the market and provides important insights into the ways of doing business and possible opportunities in the country.

Uncertainty: In many countries, the institutions of

government are still evolving and there are unsettled political questions. Companies are unwilling to contribute large amounts of capital into an environment where some of the basic political questions have not yet been resolved.

Macroeconomic Environment: Instability in the level of prices and the exchange rate makes business planning difficult and increases the level of uncertainty. This increases the perceived risk of making investments and so adversely affects the inflow of FDI.

Legal and Regulatory Framework: The transition towards a market economy entails the establishment of a legal and regulatory framework that is compatible with private sector activities and the operation of foreign-owned companies. The areas of importance in this field include protection of property rights, ability to repatriate profits, and a free market for currency exchange. It is important that these rules and their related administrative procedures are transparent and easily comprehensible.

Access to Basic Inputs: FDI can be attracted by a country through the easy availability of factors of production. Many developing countries have large reserves of skilled and semi-skilled workers that are available for employment at wages significantly lower than in developed countries. This provides an opportunity for foreign firms to make investments in these countries to cater to the export market. Availability of natural resources such as oil and gas, minerals and forestry products also determine the extent of FDI.

Foreign Exchange: It means currencies of all other countries against which the native currency can be exchanged.

Foreign Exchange Management Act (FEMA), 1999: Realising that Foreign Exchange Regulation Act (FERA), 1973 (q.v.) was not in tune with the economic reforms initiated since 1991, the Government of India replaced it with a new legislation, viz. Foreign Exchange Management Act (FEMA), 1999 which came into effect from June 1, 2000. FERA, 1973 remained a nightmare for 27 years for the Indian corporate world. The objective of the new legislation as stated in the preamble to the Act is *to facilitate external trade and payments and promote the orderly development and maintenance of the foreign exchange market in India*—a shift in the approach from *conservation of foreign exchange resources of the country and the proper utilisation thereof* under the FERA, 1973.

Under FEMA, foreign exchange law violators are treated as civil offenders rather than as criminals as was the case under FERA, 1973. Contravention of the provisions of FEMA invites monetary penalties. Moreover, FEMA provides for a number of appellate authorities who can be approached by the aggrieved party against whom penalties have been levied. A qualitative change has been brought about in the legal framework by FEMA. The objectives of regulation have been redefined as facilitating trade and payments as well as orderly development and maintenance of foreign exchange market in India. The legal framework envisages both the developmental dimension and orderliness or stability. The legislation provides power to the government to re-impose controls if public interest warrants it.

The shift in the policy approach entailed significant implications for the operations of the RBI. Under the new system, all current account payments except those notified by the government are eligible for appropriate foreign currency in respect of genuine transactions from the authorised dealers without any restrictions. The surrender requirements in respect of exports of goods and services continue to operate. The RBI would, however, have the necessary regulatory jurisdiction over capital account transactions.

Distinguishing Features of FEMA, 1999: The reforms in industrial and trade policies initiated in the early 1990s, consistent with the changing international economic and trade relations, gave rise to the need for a more conducive climate for increased inflow of foreign investment and capital to accelerate the pace of industrial growth and export promotion. The FEMA diluted the rigorous enforcement provisions of FERA, 1973. Under FEMA: (a) the prosecution has to prove the guilt of the accused person, (b) only monetary penalty is provided for contraventions, (c) contravention of FEMA provisions are dealt with under civil procedures, for which separate administrative mechanisms in the form of Compounding Rules, Adjudicating Authority, Special Director (Appeals) and Appellate Tribunal have been established, and (d) for each process of law a timeframe has been provided in the Act.

The concept of compounding is an important feature of FEMA. (Under FERA, 1973 all violations were subject to separate investigation and adjudication of the Directorate of Enforcement). The FEMA provides an opportunity of seeking compounding of contraventions, in terms of which a contravener has a *suo moto* opportunity of making an application to the compounding authority seeking the contravention to be compounded. The compounding authority is required to dispose of the application within 180 days.

The Government of India, in one of the recent Notifications, has designated the RBI as the compounding authority for all contraventions under the FEMA, except for those involving *hawala* transactions for which the Directorate of Enforcement would be the compounding authority. The new procedure provides quick and hassle-free disposal of the cases involving contravention(s) of FEMA. See also Foreign Exchange Regulation Act (FERA), 1947 and Foreign Exchange Regulation Act (FERA), 1973.

Foreign Exchange Market: It refers to market where any country's currency can be bought/sold for another country's currency. It does not refer to any geographical market.

Foreign Exchange Regulation Act (FERA), 1947: This legislation was enacted under the British regime as a temporary measure for 5 years. It was further extended for another 5 years in 1952. It was finally made a permanent Act in 1957 and it remained in force up till January 1974. The limited objective of the Act was *to regulate the inflow of foreign capital*, in view of the concerns about substantial non-resident interests and employment of foreigners. The prevailing mood in independent India was one of preserving and consolidating freedom and not permitting once again any sort of foreign domination, political or economic. The control framework was essentially transaction-based—all transactions in foreign exchange including those between residents and non-residents were prohibited, unless specifically permitted. The Second Five Year Plan with a substantial step-up in the investment on industrialisation put a heavy strain on foreign exchange resources. Exports were not picking up while imports were surging, aggravating the balance of payments crisis.

The Act empowered the RBI, and in certain cases the Central Government, to control and regulate dealing in foreign exchange payment outside India, export and import of currency notes and bullion, transfers of securities between residents and non-residents, acquisition of foreign securities etc.

The stance of foreign exchange policy during the 1950s was to manage the exchange rate mainly for facilitating India's imports. The strict foreign exchange control had the dubious distinction of creating a wide unofficial market for foreign currencies. See also Foreign Exchange Regulation Act (FERA), 1973; and Foreign Exchange Management Act (FEMA), 1999.

Foreign Exchange Regulation Act (FERA), 1973: The uncertainties in the global economy following the breakdown of the Bretton Woods system of stable exchange rates and the emergence of the floating regimes exacerbated by the oil shock of 1973-74 presented serious challenges for exchange rate management and gave rise to balance of payments difficulties in India as in many other developing countries.

In view of the above and following the recommendations of the Public Accounts Committee concerning the leakage of foreign exchange through invoice manipulation (June 1971) and the Report of the Law Commission on 'Trial and Punishment of Social and Economic Offences' (April 1972), Government of

India reviewed Foreign Exchange Regulation Act (FERA), 1947 (q.v.) *for conserving foreign exchange rather than regulating the entry of foreign capital*. The FERA, 1973 was drafted with the objective of introducing the changes necessary for effective implementation of the Government policy and removing the difficulties in the working of the previous enactment.

As a crisis-driven legislation, the FERA, 1973 naturally contained several draconian provisions. Any offence under the FERA was a criminal offence liable for imprisonment. Under this controversial piece of legislation, foreign exchange law violators (which included sometimes big names in Indian industry) were treated as criminals and dealt with sternly. Severe restrictions on current account transactions continued till the mid-1990s when relaxations were made in the operations of the legislation of 1973 to enable convertibility on current account.

The control framework was equally valid for the capital account, though the capital account was negligible till the 1980s. Most receipts on capital account were on Government account and through external assistance in addition to the bilateral arrangement with erstwhile USSR. In the 1980s, there were significant private capital flows through external commercial borrowings (ECBs) and deposits from non-resident Indians (NRIs). The position changed in the 1990s, with gradual liberalisation of the capital account.

The FERA empowered the central Government to give to the RBI such general or special directions as it thought fit and the RBI was obliged to comply with these directions in discharge of its functions under the Act. To a large extent, the exchange control related to and supplemented by the trade control administered by the Chief Controller of Imports and Exports in the Ministry of Commerce of the Government of India. Exchange controls had a wider scope *vis-à-vis* the trade controls, as it involved supervision over the settlement of financial transactions in respect of all exports and imports as also invisibles and capital transactions, whereas trade control was concerned with the physical transfer of goods (mostly confined to imports). The major functions of the RBI relating to exchange control included granting licenses to certain scheduled commercial banks to deal in foreign exchange (authorised dealers); and issuing directions to the authorised dealers and other entities (airline, shipping companies, travel agents and insurance companies) in matters concerning their operations having foreign exchange implications. See also Foreign Exchange Regulation Act (FERA), 1947, and Foreign Exchange Management Act (FEMA), 1999.

Forged Cheque: A cheque on which the drawer's signature has been forged.

Forgery: The fraudulent signing or alteration of another's name to an instrument such as a deed, mortgage, or cheque. The intent of the forgery is to deceive or defraud.

Forward Exchange Rate: A forward exchange rate is the price set between two parties for delivery of a foreign currency on an agreed future date.

Forwards/Forward Contracts: A forward contract is a particularly simple derivative. A deal for the purchase or sale of a commodity, security or other asset can be in the spot or forward markets. A spot or cash market is the most commonly used for trading. A majority of day to day transaction are in the cash market, where we pay cash and get the delivery of the goods. In addition to a cash purchase, another way to acquire or sell assets is by entering into a forward contract. In a forward contract, the buyer agrees to pay cash at a later date when the seller delivers the goods.

A forward contract is an agreement to buy or sell an asset on a specified date for a specified price. One of the parties to the contract assumes a long position and agrees to buy the underlying asset on a certain specified future date for a certain specified price. The other party assumes a short position and agrees to sell the asset on the same date for the same price. Other contract details like delivery date, price and quantity are negotiated bilaterally by the parties to the contract. The forward contracts are normally traded outside the exchanges.

Salient Features of Forward Contracts: These are as under:

1. They are bilateral contracts and hence exposed to counterparty risk.
2. Each contract is custom designed, and hence is unique in terms of contract size, expiration date and the asset type and quality.
3. Contract price is generally not available in public domain.
4. On the expiration date, the contract has to be settled by delivery of the asset.
5. If the party wishes to reverse the contract, it has to compulsorily go to the same counterparty, which often results in high prices being charged.

Usually no money changes hands when forward contracts are entered into, but sometimes one or both the parties to a contract may like to ask for some initial, good-faith deposits to insure that the contract is honoured by the other party.

A forward contract is settled at maturity. The holder of the short position delivers the asset to the holder price. A forward contract is worth zero when it is first entered into. Later it can have position or negative value, depending on movements in the price of the asset.

However, forward contracts in certain markets have become much standardised, as in the case of foreign exchange, thereby reducing transaction costs and increasing transaction volumes. This process of standardisation reaches its limit in the organised futures market.

Advantages of Forwards: Forward contracts are very useful in hedging and speculation. A typical hedging application would be that of an exporter who expects to receive payment in dollars 3 months later. He is exposed to the risk of exchange rate fluctuations. By using the currency forward market to sell dollars forward, he can lock-on to a rate today and reduce his uncertainty. Similarly, an importer who is required to make a payment in dollars 2 months hence can reduce his exposure to exchange rate fluctuations by buying dollars forward.

In a forward contract the price at which the underlying commodity or assets will be traded, is decided at the time of entering into the contract. The essential idea of entering into the forward contract is to peg the price and thereby avoid the price risk. Thus by entering in the forward contract, one is assured of the price at which one can buy/sell goods or other assets. Manufacturers using a certain raw material whose price is subject to variation, can avoid the risk of price moving adversely by entering into a forward contract and plan their operations better. Similarly, by entering into a forward contract, a farmer can ensure the price he can get for his crops and not worry about what price would prevail at the time of maturity of the contract. Of course, at the time of maturity of contract, if the market price of the commodity is greater than the price agreed, then the buyer stands to gain. The opposite would hold when the market price is lower than the agreed price.

If a speculator has information or analysis, which forecasts an upturn in a price, then he can go long on the forward market instead of the cash market. The speculator would go long on the forward, wait for the price to rise, and then take a reversing transaction to book profits. Speculators may well be required to deposit a margin upfront. However, this is generally a relatively small proportion of the value of the assets underlying the forward contract. The use of forward markets provides leverage to the speculator.

Problems of Forward Contracts: A forward contract is evidently a good mean of avoiding price risk, but it entails elements of risk in that a party to the contract may not honour its part of the obligation. Thus, each party is at risk of default. There is another problem. Once a position of buyer and seller takes in a forward contract, an investor cannot retreat except through mutual consent with the party or by entering into an identical contract and taking a position that is the reverse of earlier position. Alternatives are by no means easy. With forward contract entered on a one-to- one basis and with no standardization, the forward contract has virtually no liquidity. This problem of credit risk and no liquidity associated with forward contracts led to the emergence of future contracts. Future contracts are the refined version of forward contracts.

Forward markets world-wide are afflicted by several problems:

1. Lack of centralisation of trading.
2. Illiquidity.
3. Counterparty risk.

In the first two of these, the basic problem is that of too much flexibility and generality. The forward market is like a real estate market in that any two consenting adults can form contracts against each other. This often makes them design terms of the deal which are very convenient in that specific situation, but makes the contract non-tradable. Counterparty risk arises from the possibility of default by any one party to the transaction. When one of the two sides to the transaction declares bankruptcy, the other suffers. Even when forward markets trade standardised contracts, and hence avoid the problem of illiquidity, still the counterparty risk remains a very serious issue.

Fraud: Frauds have been classified as under, based mainly on the provisions of the Indian Penal Code:

1. Misappropriation and criminal breach of trust.
2. Fraudulent encashment through forged instruments, manipulation of books of account or through fictitious accounts and conversion of property.
3. Unauthorised credit facilities extended for reward or for illegal gratification.
4. Negligence and cash shortages.
5. Cheating and forgery.
6. Irregularities in foreign exchange transactions.
7. Any other type of fraud not coming under the specific heads as above.

Free on Board (FOB): It is a price quotation indicating that the seller is responsible for all costs of shipment of goods, including responsibility for damage or loss, up to a certain named point. For example, FOB buyer's plant means the seller is responsible for the cost of the goods and their transportation and arrival in good condition at the buyer's plant.

Free-trade Zone: See Duty-free Zone, *68*.

Fringe Benefit: It is an indirect, non-cash benefit provided to employees by employers in addition to regular wage or salary compensation, such as health insurance, life insurance, profit-sharing, and the like.

Frozen Account: An account on which funds may not be withdrawn until a lien is satisfied and a court order or other legal process makes the account available for withdrawal. For example, the account of a deceased person is frozen pending a court order distributing the funds to the new lawful owners. An account may also be frozen when there is a dispute regarding the true ownership of an account. The bank will freeze the account to preserve the existing funds until legal action can determine the lawful owner.

Functions of a Commercial Bank: See Commercial Bank, *37*.

Functions of Money: See Money, *155*.

Future Trading: It refers to commodity or currency trading done on contract for future delivery. The purpose is to insure against risks of price changes, exchange rate changes etc. or to make a profit by speculating on the price trends.

Futures/Future Contracts: Future markets are designed to solve the problems that exist in forward markets. A future contract is an agreement between two parties to buy or sell an asset at a certain time in future at a certain price. However, unlike forward contracts, the future contracts are standardised and exchange traded. To facilitate liquidity in the future contracts, the exchange specifies certain standard features of the contract. It is a standardised contract with standard underlying instrument, a standard quantity and quality of the underlying instrument that can be delivered and a standard timing of such settlement.

A future contract may be offset prior to maturity by entering into an equal and opposite transaction. The standardised items in a future contract are as under:

1. Quantity of the underlying.
2. Quality of the underlying.
3. Date and the month of delivery.
4. Units of price quotation and minimum price change.
5. Location of settlement.

Future contracts are normally traded on an exchange. To make trading possible, the exchange specifies certain standardized features of the contract. As the two parties to the contract do not necessarily know each other the exchange also provides a mechanism, which gives the two parties a guarantee that the contract will be honoured.

Distinction between Futures and Forwards: Forward and future contracts are different in following respects.

Standardization: A forward contract is a tailor-made contract between the buyer and the seller where the terms are settled in mutual agreement between the parties. On the other hand, a future contract is standardized in regards to the quality, quantity, place of delivery of the asset etc. Only the price is negotiated. Forwards are popular on the over the counter (OTC) market. Futures are traded on an organised stock exchange. Exchange-traded derivatives tend to be more standardised and offer greater liquidity than OTC contracts, which are negotiated between counterparties and tailored to meet the needs of the parties to the contract. Exchange-traded derivatives also offer centralised limits on individual positions and have formal rules for risk and burden sharing.

Liquidity: There is no secondary market for forward contracts while future contracts are traded on organized exchanges.

Accordingly, future contracts are usually much more liquid than the forward contracts. Forwards have customised contract terms, and therefore they are less liquid. Futures have standardised contract terms, and hence they are more liquid.

Conclusion of Contract: A forward contract is generally concluded with a delivery of the asset in question whereas the future contracts are settled sometimes with delivery of the asset and generally with the payment of the price differences. One who holds a contract can always eliminate his/her obligation by subsequently selling a contract for the same asset and same delivery date, before the conclusion of contract one holds. In the same manner, the seller of a future contract can buy a similar contract and offset his/her position before maturity of the first contract. Each one of these actions is called offsetting a trade.

Margins: A forward contract has zero value for both the parties involved so that no collateral is required for entering into such a contract. There are only two parties involved. But in a futures contract, a third party called Clearing Corporation is also involved with which margin is required to be kept by both parties. In other words, forwards require no margin payments. Futures require margin payments.

Profit/Loss Settlement: The settlement of a forward contract takes place on the date of maturity so that the profit/loss is booked on maturity only. On the other hand, the future contracts are marked-to-market daily so that the profits or losses are settled daily. In other words, in the case of forwards, settlement happens at the end of the period. Futures follow daily settlement.

Thus, future contracts are a significant improvement over forward contracts as they eliminate counterparty risk and offer more liquidity.

Future contracts represent an improvement over the forward contracts in terms of standardization, performance guarantee and liquidity. A future contract is a standardized contract between two parties where one of the parties commits to sell, and the other to buy, a stipulated quantity of a commodity, currency, security, index or some other specified item at an agreed price on a given date in the future.

Future contracts are traded on commodity exchanges or other future exchanges. People can buy or sell futures like other commodities. When an investor buys a future contract on an organized future exchange, he is in fact assuming the right and obligation of taking the delivery of the specified underlying item on a specified date. Similarly, when an investor sells a contract, to take a short position, one assumes the right and obligation to make the delivery of the underlying asset. There is no risk of non-performance in the case of trading in the future contracts. This is because a clearing house or a clearing corporation is associated with the futures exchange, which plays a pivotal role in the trading of futures. A clearing house takes the opposite in each trade, so that it becomes the buyer to the seller and vice versa. When a party takes a short position in a contract, it is obliged to sell the underlying commodity in question at the stipulated price to the clearing house on maturity of the contract. Similarly, an investor who takes a long position on the contract can seek its performance through the clearing house only.

It is noteworthy that while a clearing house guarantees the performance of the future contracts, the parties in the contracts are required to keep margins with it. The margins are taken to ensure that each party to a contract performs its part. The margins are adjusted on a daily basis to account for the gains or losses, depending upon the situation. This is known as marking-to-market and involves giving a credit to the buyer of the contract, if the price of the contract rises, debiting the seller's account by an equal amount. Similarly, the buyer's balance is reduced when the contract price declines and the seller's account is accordingly updated.

It is not necessary to hold on to a futures contract until maturity and one can easily close out a position. Either of the parties may reverse their position by initiating a reverse trade, so that the original buyer of a contract can sell an identical contract at a later date, cancelling, in effect, the original contract. Thus, the exchange facilitates subsequent selling (buying) of a contract so that a party can offset its position and eliminate the obligation. The fact that the buyer as well as the seller of a contract is free to transfer his interest in the contract to another party makes such contracts highly liquid in nature. In fact, most of the future contracts are cancelled by the parties, by engaging into reverse trades: the buyers cancel a contract by selling another contract, while the seller does so by buying another contract. Only a very small portion of them is held for actual delivery.

Introduction of Futures in India: The first derivative product introduced in the Indian securities market was *index futures* in June 2000. In India, the *stock futures* were first introduced on November 9, 2001.

The Indian capital market has grown quite well since the early 1990s. In the boom period of 1992 and thereafter, even the common man was attracted to the stock market. The stock market was considered a profitable investment opportunity. Before July 2001, various stock exchanges including the Bombay Stock Exchange (BSE), National Stock Exchange (NSE) and Delhi Stock Exchange, provided carry forward facilities through the traditional *badla* system. By means of this system the purchase or sale of a security was not postponed till a particular future date; instead the system only provided for the carry forward of a transaction from one settlement period (seven days) to the next settlement period for the payment of a fee known as *badla* charges.

In the *badla* system, due to limited settlement period and no future price discovery, a speculator could manipulate prices, thus causing loss to small investors and ultimately eroding investors' confidence in the capital market. Hence, the necessity of futures trading in the capital market was emphasized. In the absence of an efficient futures market, there was no price discovery and therefore prices could be moved in any desired direction. Recent developments in the capital market culminated in a ban on *badla* from July 2001.

In the absence of futures trading, certain operators—either on their own or in collusion with corporate management teams—at times manipulated prices in the secondary market, causing irreparable damage to the growth of the market. The small and medium investors, who are the backbone of the market and whose savings come to the market via primary or secondary routes shied away. As the small investors avoided the capital market, the downturn in the secondary market ultimately affected the primary market because people stopped investing in share for fear of loss or liquidity. Introducing futures in major shares along with index futures helped to revive the capital market. This not only provided liquidity and efficiency to the market, but also helped in future price discovery.

Futures and Stock Indices: For understanding stock index futures a thorough knowledge of the composition of indexes is essential. Choosing the right index is important in choosing the right contract for speculation or hedging. For speculation, the volatility of the index is important whereas for hedging the choice of index depends upon the relationship between the stocks being hedged and the characteristics of the index.

Choosing and understanding the right index is important as the movement of stock index futures is quite similar to that of the underlying stock index. Volatility of the future indexes is generally greater than spot stock indexes.

Every time an investor takes a long or short position on a stock, he also has hidden exposure to the Nifty or Sensex. This is so because most often stock values fall in tune with the entire market sentiment and rise when the market as a whole is rising.
Retail investors will find the index derivatives useful due to the high correlation of the index with their portfolio/stock and low cost associated with using index futures for hedging.

Index Futures: A future contract is an agreement between two parties to buy or sell an asset at a certain time in the future at a certain price. Index futures are all future contracts where the underlying is the stock index (Nifty or Sensex) and helps a trader to take a view of the market as a whole.

Index futures permit speculation and if a trader anticipates a major rally in the market, he can simply buy a future contract and hope for a price rise on the future contract when the rally occurs.

Settlements in the Futures Market: All trades in the futures market are cash settled on a T+1 basis and all positions (buy/sell) which are not closed out are marked-to-market. The closing price of the index futures is the daily settlement price and the position is carried to the next day at the settlement price.

The most common way of liquidating an open position is to execute an offsetting future transaction by which the initial transaction is squared up. The initial buyer liquidates his long position by selling identical future contract. In index futures the other way of settlement is cash settled at the final settlement. At the end of the contract period the difference between the contract value and closing index value is paid.

Gg

Garnishment/Garnish: A legal process that allows a creditor to remove funds from your bank account to satisfy a debt that you have not paid. If you owe money to a person or company, they can obtain a court order directing your bank to take money out of your account to pay off your debt.

General Insurance Corporation of India (GIC): It was established when the general insurance business was nationalised in India with effect from January 1, 1973.

Gilt-edged Security: A term used to describe a bond, generally issued by the government, or issued with a government guarantee, so much so that there are no doubts about the ability of the issuer to pay regular interest and the principal amount to the bond holders.

Globalisation: Globalisation implies widening and deepening integration with the *globe*, i.e. with people and processes abroad. Further, at the end of the integrative effort there must lie some concrete benefits for the country, for otherwise the globalisation being attempted would not be worth the effort. The trend towards the evolution of a global society is generally thought of in economic terms and in terms of the consequences of the revolution in communication technologies.

There is undoubtedly much greater economic integration among the nations of the world today. Globalisation is widely seen as the most important factor that could influence economies of nations the world over in the new millennium. The rapid advancement in information technology and communications has made it not just possible but absolutely essential for industry the world over to adapt or fall by the wayside.

Gold Exchange Standard: It refers to a system which emerged after World War II featuring a fixed exchange rate policy defined in terms of gold. The rate of exchange was allowed to fluctuate within a narrow range around its official parity. This system was a mixture of gold exchange and reserve currency standard.

Gold Standard: This system operated during 1870 to 1914 and then during 1925 to 1931. It provided for almost fixed rates of exchange. Under this, all national governments were committed to buy and sell a specified amount of gold for a specified amount of their currency. Thus, if all countries did alike, the rate of exchange between them could be determined by the ratio of the gold parities.

Prior to 1914, gold standard was a type of monetary system with the following characteristics: the national monetary unit was defined in terms of a given quantity of gold; the central bank or treasury stood ready to buy and sell gold at the resulting fixed price in terms of the national currency; gold was freely coined and gold coin formed a significant part of the circulating medium; and gold could be freely exported and imported. The exchange rate between any two countries adhering to such arrangements was determined by the gold content of their respective monetary units and could vary from this parity only within a narrow band (the gold points) reflecting the cost of shipping gold from one country to the other. Private arbitrage shipments of gold, which became profitable when either of these limits was reached, prevented the band from being breached.

The objective of economic policy under the pre-1914 gold standard was to maintain the redeemability (convertibility) of the national currency directly or indirectly into gold at the legal parity, i.e. to keep exchange rates fixed against other gold standard currencies. From about 1880 to 1914, exchange rates among gold standard countries remained fixed without support of payments or import controls, with virtually no countries being forced off the gold standard once adopted.

During the First World War, most countries suspended the redeemability of their currencies into gold, withdrew gold coins from circulation, and concentrated gold holdings in official reserves. The currencies of most belligerent countries did not, however, depreciate by much in terms of gold and the dollar because of official pegging operations supported by gold sales, foreign borrowing, liquidation of assets abroad, and imposition of some import and exchange controls. At the end of the War, USA was virtually the only country on a full gold standard.

After the War, governments were eager to return to the gold standard at an early date. This was a laborious process that was not generally completed until 1927 because of the widespread economic dislocations that followed the War. In some cases the return to gold involved stabilisation of the currency at the pre-War parity, the most notable example being that of Great Britain in 1925. In other cases, such as that of France, Italy, and Belgium, currencies were re-pegged to gold at only a fraction of their pre-War parities. In those countries where hyperinflation had occurred in the early post-War years, notably in Germany, the stabilisation process necessitated the introduction of completely new currencies.

The international gold standard that was restored in the mid-1920s differed in several respects from that of the pre-1914 period. Apart from in the US, the gold coin standard had virtually disappeared, and gold holdings remained predominantly in official hands. Several countries, including Great Britain, adopted a so-called gold bullion standard under which the currency was redeemable in gold but only in the form of bars of a minimum weight. This, in effect, made gold available only for purposes of settling international balances. The great majority of countries, partly in view of a prevailing belief in an actual or impending world shortage of gold, adopted varieties of the gold exchange standard.

International gold standard, which for the most part was a gold exchange standard, broke down in 1930 to 1932 under the impact of the world depression, the virtual cessation of international lending, the massive liquidation by central banks of their foreign exchange holdings, and the large-scale flights of capital from individual countries. Great Britain abandoned gold standard in September 1931 and US suspended it in March 1933.

Grants: Grants are unilateral transfers from one level of government to another (usually lower) level of government. They have the advantage of being targeted towards fiscally disadvantaged state/municipal governments to reduce horizontal fiscal imbalances. They can also be made conditional regarding their utilisation. Keeping in mind the criteria of fiscal equity and efficiency, three types of grants may be given by a higher level government to a lower level government.

1. General purpose (or unconditional) grants are given to offset fiscal disadvantages arising from lower taxable capacity and/or higher unit cost of the services provided (due to bad terrain etc.). Such equalising grants have to be general and their basic purpose is to enable different municipalities to come up to a minimum standard of services provided.
2. Specific purpose (or conditional) grants are tied to the achievement of specific objectives. They may be with or without matching requirements. They are used to ensure minimum levels of specified public services to be provided by municipalities. Such grants are justified also where municipal services have spillover effects. Thus, afforestation, slum improvement, and literacy drives create benefits not only for the local residents but also for the community as a whole. Such schemes should preferably be financed through grants from the state to municipalities.
3. Incentive grants are given for the purpose of encouraging municipalities to streamline their operations. These grants should depend on the measures taken by the municipalities to strengthen their financial position.

Great Depression: In the early years of 1930s, US and other capitalist countries of the world suffered a business depression of extraordinary severity. The demand for goods fell sharply and so also the prices. Many business firms failed and million of workers were rendered unemployed. These events revealed that something was seriously wrong with the working of a capitalist system. Out of the turmoil of depression came a book that had a profound effect on the thinking of economists. It was titled *The General Theory of Employment, Interest and Money* (1936) authored by British economist John Maynard Keynes (1883-1946). This work was immediately recognised as a revolutionary landmark in the history of economic ideas. See also Keynesian Economics.

Grey Market: It refers to a market in which commodities in short supply are sold for immediate delivery at exorbitant prices, taking unfair advantage of a crisis situation.

Guarantor: A party who agrees to be responsible for the payment of another party's debts should that party default.

Hh

Hacking: It refers to the practice of breaking into a computer without authorisation, for malicious reasons, just to prove it can be done, or for other personal reasons.

Hard Currency: See Currency, *54*.

Hedging: It is a method to guard against fluctuations in the prices of commodities (particularly raw materials) scheduled for future delivery by dealing in futures market. *Buying hedge* and *selling hedge* are the two basic types of hedge operations.

A baker, for example, might buy a quantity of flour to convert it into bread at a given point in time and agree at the same time to sell a similar quantity of flour that he does not own, at the same price, for delivery at a designated future point in time. If the price of flour falls, he will lose on the bread while making a profit on the flour he can later buy at the lower price. However, if the price of flour rises, he will make an extra profit on his bread, which he will have to sacrifice by purchasing flour at the current high price. In either case, his production profits are protected.

High-powered Money: It is composed of cash in the hands of the public, bank reserves and clearing balances held by the commercial banks with the central bank.

Hoarding: It refers to an act of accumulation. Dishoarding is the reverse of it, signifying spending.

Hold: Used to indicate that a certain amount of a customer's balance may not be withdrawn until an item has been collected, or until a specific cheque or debit is posted.

Hot Money: The term refers to money which can be transferred rapidly from one financial centre to another to take advantage of differences in short-term interest rates.

Human Capital: It refers to health, strength, education, training, and skills that people bring to their jobs.

Hypothecation: It means pledging of property to secure a debt, without giving up possession of such property.

Ii

IMF: See International Monetary Fund, *133*.

Import Duty: See Customs Duty, *56*.

Imputed Income: Imputed income arises when one is himself the producer and the consumer of a given commodity or service as, for example, imputed rent from owner-occupied residence. Although no market transaction is involved yet the owner enjoys a certain amount of consumption. Fringe benefits (like subsidised or free accommodation available to company executives) are also examples of imputed income. There are two difficulties with imputed incomes: (a) they accrue in kind, and (b) they are not the result of a market transaction.

Inactive Account: An account that has little or no activity; neither deposits nor withdrawals having been posted to the account for a significant period of time.

Index-linked Certificate of Deposit (CD): An index-linked CD is a deposit obligation of the issuing bank and is often sold through bank branches and affiliated and unaffiliated brokers. Index-linked CDs provide the investor the ability to participate in the appreciation, if any, of a particular index, during the term of the CD. Index-linked CDs may have complicated payout structures and may not be suitable or appropriate for all investors. Investors should carefully review the investment risk considerations detailed in the relevant offering documents and disclosure statements. Index-linked CDs are not securities and are not registered under securities laws.

India Infrastructure Finance Company Limited (IIFCL)

IIFCL was incorporated on January 5, 2006 with a paid up capital of ₹ 10 crore and an authorized capital of ₹ 1,000 crore.

Apart from its equity, IIFCL is funded through long-term debt raised from the open market. To enable the company to do so, the Government extends a guarantee for repayment of principal and interest. The extent of guarantee provided by Government of India in the first year of operations was ₹ 10,000 crore.

The setting up of IIFCL as a wholly owned Government company redeemed the promise made in the Budget Speech for 2005-06. There were many infrastructure projects which were financially viable but, in the current situation, faced difficulties in raising resources. It was proposed that such projects in specified sectors—roads, ports, airports and tourism—be funded through a financial special purpose vehicle (SPV). The SPV would lend funds especially debt of longer term maturity, directly to the eligible projects to supplement other loans from banks and financial institutions Government communicates the borrowing limit to the SPV at the beginning of each fiscal year. For 2005-06, the borrowing limit was fixed at ₹ 10,000 crore.

IIFCL is a SPV created in keeping with the announcement made by the Finance Minister in his Budget Speech for the year 2005-06. The company renders financial assistance through the following channels:

1. Direct lending to eligible projects.
2. Refinance to banks and financial institutions (FIs) for loans with period of 5 years or more.
3. Any other method approved by the Government of India.

The other salient features of infrastructure funding through the company are as under:

1. Loan assistance from SPV shall not exceed 20 percent of project cost.
2. A project awarded to a private sector company for development, financing, construction through PPP shall have overriding priority under the scheme.
3. Private sector companies will not be eligible for direct lending and only the refinancing option will be available in such cases. Further, the total lending to such projects will be kept within 20 percent of the lending programme of the IIFCL.

4. The rate of interest charged by IIFCL shall be such as to cover all fund costs including guarantee fee as well as administrative cost.

IIFCL is expected to be a very lean organization which would keep overheads to the minimum and thus keep the cost of funds for infrastructure at a competitive level. The company would fill the gap for long term infrastructure finance which the banks are not in a position to address owing to concerns relating to mismatches in assets and liabilities.

Indirect Tax: It is a tax which can be shifted from the original payer to the ultimate consumer of the commodity or service taxed. Import duties, excise levies, and sales taxes are generally regarded as indirect taxes. Thus, an excise duty on cigarettes levied on producers is usually passed on to the consumers in the form of higher prices.

Indirect taxes (also called hidden taxes) are convenient to collect but lack equity attribute. They do not allow considerations for the personal circumstances of taxpayers as do direct taxes. It is not possible to grant exemptions or allow deductions or to have a progressive rate schedule. Indirect taxes are borne in relation to the consumption expenditure which constitutes a higher percentage of income for lower income groups than for persons in higher income brackets. It is true that incidence of indirect taxes depends on: (a) the selection of commodities for taxation, and (b) the rate of tax on them. It is desirable that luxuries and comforts are chosen for heavy taxation with necessities of life either exempted or moderately taxed. However, in poor countries the demand for luxury items is limited apart from being price elastic. Conversely, the demand for necessities is vast and price inelastic, obliging tax authorities to extend the tax net to daily needs. This has a tendency to fuel inflation.

In short, it is almost universally accepted that indirect taxes are inferior to direct taxes in terms of equity attribute. The distribution of indirect tax burden is often, though not always, regressive and even the poorest of the poor are made to contribute to public exchequer. See also Direct Tax.

Individual Account: An account in the name of one individual.

Individual Retirement Account (IRA): A retirement savings programme for individuals to which yearly tax-deductible contributions up to a specified limit can be made. The amount contributed is not taxed until withdrawn. Withdrawal is not permitted without penalty until the individual reaches a specified age.

Industrial Credit and Investment Corporation of India Ltd. (ICICI): It was established as a public limited company in 1955 to encourage and assist industrial concerns in the country. ICICI is a private sector institution which provides term loans in rupees and foreign currencies, underwrites issues of shares and debentures, and makes direct subscriptions to these issues. It is noteworthy that ICICI was merged with ICICI Bank on March 30, 2002.

Industrial Development Bank of India (IDBI): It is the principal financial institution for providing credit and other facilities for the development of industry. Set up under the Industrial Development Bank of India Act, 1964, it co-ordinates the working of institutions engaged in financing, promoting industries and for assisting the development of such institutions. It provides direct financial assistance to large and medium industrial concerns and helps small industries through State level financial institutions. It is the apex organisation in the field of development banking. It may be noted that IDBI was established as a subsidiary of the RBI. However, it was delinked from the RBI in 1976 and was converted into a holding company.

Taking into account the changing operating environment following the initiation of economic reforms in the early 1990s, the Government decided to transform IDBI into a commercial bank without eschewing its traditional development finance obligations. It was thought that migration to the new business model of commercial banking, with its access to low cost current/saving bank deposits, would enable it to overcome most of the limitations of the current model of development finance.

Industrial Finance: Modern system of industrial production is very complex requiring huge investments both in terms of material and human resources. It may be beyond the capacity of an individual to arrange on his own all the resources required to undertake production. Modern corporations or joint stock companies are the answer to these requirements. Financial needs of a modern industry may be classified into two categories: (a) fixed capital, and (b) working capital. Modern industry is capital-intensive by nature and its fixed capital includes lands and buildings, plant and machinery, and tools and implements. The requirement of finance to purchase fixed capital is essentially long-term in nature. The working capital, short-term in nature, is required to purchase raw materials and meet day-to-day administrative and other such expenses.

There are various sources of finance for a modern industrial unit. These sources are of two types: (a) internal sources, and (b) external sources. Internal sources include paid-up capital in the form of share subscriptions, ploughing back of profits, and reserves. The external sources include debenture issue, public deposits, loans from commercial banks and other specialised institutions.

Industrial Finance Corporation of India (IFCI): It was set up in 1948 by an Act of Parliament with the objective of meeting the medium and long-term credit needs of industrial concerns in the country. Its establishment marked the begging of the era of development banking in India. Being the first such institutions in the post-Independence period, it has undertaken a wide range of promotional activities.

Industrial Investment Bank of India (IIBI): In 1971, Industrial Reconstruction Corporation of India (IRCI) Ltd. was jointly set up by IDBI, LIC and banks to look after the rehabilitation of sick units. It was renamed as the Industrial Reconstruction Bank of

India (IRBI) in 1984. It was converted into a full-fledged public financial institution in 1997 and was renamed as the Industrial Investment Bank of India (IIBI).

Inflation: Inflation means a significant rise in the general price level in a country over a long period of time. Inflation is the opposite of price stability. In economics, price stability is not used in a rigid sense to mean price fixity. A modest increase of 2 to 3 percent in the price level per annum is compatible, sometimes even desirable, with the general connotation of price stability. However, when the general price rise is appreciable, say in double-digit figure, and experienced over a long period of time, it gets the dreaded name inflation.

Changes in the level of prices are measured by means of index numbers. The index of prices includes a wide variety of goods and services which are essential for life. Since the relative importance of different goods in the family budget is not the same therefore each commodity included in the index is assigned a weight in accordance with the proportion of family expenditure on that commodity. The prices of different commodities multiplied by their respective weights give the aggregate for the year chosen as the base. This is then compared with the similar aggregate of prices in some subsequent year for the purpose of comparison. The base year is changed from time to time to accommodate new products and reflect current economic conditions.

Analysis of price variations is essential to understand the general economic conditions and the value of money in the economy. Price fluctuations influence: (a) the distribution of income among various economic classes, and (b) the allocation of resources among competing sectors. Hence, their analysis indicates as to what regulatory policies by the government are needed as corrective measures. Price stability is a pre-requisite for a successful development strategy.

Pressure on prices is a manifestation of macro-imbalance between demand for and supply of commodities and services. Inflation signifies excess of demand for goods and services over their available supply. It is a case of too much money chasing too few goods.

The reasons for excess of demand over supply are many. Demand may expand due to any combination of the following factors: (a) increase in population leading to increased demand for essential items, (b) increase in government expenditure, particularly when it is met by deficit financing and the consequent monetary expansion, and (c) increase in private conspicuous consumption due to tax evasion and violation of economic regulations.

Supply may lag behind demand due to: (a) unfavourable and uncertain weather conditions, (b) outmoded technology, and (c) lack of infrastructural facilities.

The distortionary effects of inflation are injurious to the smooth functioning of an economy. Therefore, price stability is a prime concern of the governments the world over. Excessive price rise causes economic distortions and social unrest, threatening political stability. Price stability is, therefore, at the root of socio-politico orderliness.

Fluctuations in the general level of prices cause corresponding changes in the value or purchasing power of money. When prices are high, the value of money is low and vice versa. Fluctuating price level causes major disturbances in the economy. Rising prices adversely affect the economic conditions of fixed income groups, particularly wage-earners. There is always a lag between price rise and money wage adjustment. Poor people in the unorganised sector are hit the worst because their incomes are not linked with price index. However, the business firms gain during price rise because the money value of goods in their stock rises continually.

Fluctuating prices generate opposite effects on debtors and creditors. Rising prices prove beneficial for debtors at the expense of creditors. Thus, inflation discourages people to invest in financial assets. Conversely, falling prices make it difficult for debtors to meet their obligations.

Judicious demand and supply management policies are

required to counteract inflationary tendencies. The main elements of strategy on the demand side include restrictive monetary policy and control of public and private expenditure. Supply management includes fuller utilisation of and addition to existing capacities. This would require adequate and timely availability of power, raw materials and transport facilities.

Inheritance Tax: It is a levy on persons who receive property upon the death of a benefactor. It is different from Estate Duty (q.v.) which is based on the value of the entire estate left behind by a decedent and before it is divided among the heirs. A tax on each inheritance to which the estate gives rise is known as inheritance tax or succession duty.

Ability-to-pay principle provides theoretical justification for the imposition of inheritance tax because a bequest of property creates an ability on the part of the inheritor to contribute to public exchequer. The tax is justified because it prevents the formation of a permanent moneyed group which can live on property handed down from generation to generation.

Inheritance taxes are generally progressive. The rate of tax increases as the relationship of the heir to the deceased grows more remote. There are usually fairly high exemptions from the tax.

Inland Bill of Lading: See Bill of Lading, *22*.

Insufficient Funds: It is a situation when a depositor's cheque account balance is inadequate to pay a cheque presented for payment.

Intangible Asset: See Asset, *8*.

Inter-corporate Dividends: These are dividends received by a company from another company. Income tax laws generally treat a parent (or a holding) company and its subsidiary company as separate legal entities and therefore tax them separately. Thus, if a holding company receives dividends from its subsidiary, the former has to pay tax on such dividends. Taxation of inter-corporate earnings is designed to prevent concentration of economic power in the hands of corporate giants.

However, this provision is said to give rise to treble taxation of such dividends, first in the hands of the earning company, then in the hands of the receiving company, and finally in the hands of individual shareholders. Tax laws often provide certain concessions to facilitate inter-corporate investment. In India, prior to the assessment year 1991-92, the adverse situation was partially remedied by Section 80M of the Income Tax Act, 1961, under which a company was entitled to a deduction of 60 percent of dividend received by it from another domestic company. An important change was introduced from the assessment year 1991-92 under which dividends received by a domestic company from another domestic company are now exempt to the full extent to which the assessee company itself distributes dividends during the relevant period. Business community has complained that this arrangement has forced companies to declare dividends. It favours complete exemption of inter-corporate dividends from tax.

Interest: Interest is defined as a payment made or received for the use of money. It is calculated as a percentage of the principal amount, payable annually. Rate of interest is important because it affects saving and investment decisions of the people in an economy.

Interest Rate: The amount paid by a borrower to a lender in exchange for the use of the lender's money for a certain period of time. Interest is paid on loans or on debt instruments, such as notes or bonds, either at regular intervals or as part of a lump sum payment when the issue matures.

Interest Rate Swap (IRS): IRS is a contract between two counter-parties for exchange interest payment for a specified period based on a notional principal amount. The notional principal is used to calculate interest payments, but is not exchanged. Only interest payments are exchanged.

International Bank for Reconstruction and Development IBRD): See World Bank, *227*.

International Development Association (IDA): See World Bank, *227*.

International Finance Corporation (IFC): See World Bank, *227*.

International Monetary Fund (IMF): IMF was established to promote international monetary co-operation through a permanent institution which provides the machinery for consultation and collaboration on international monetary problems. Specifically, the function of the IMF is to promote orderly and stable foreign currency exchange markets, to facilitate international trade and to contribute to balance of payments adjustment. To further these objectives, the IMF makes financial resources available to its member countries in times of balance of payments difficulties.

The IMF's charter embodied in the Articles of Agreement was agreed upon at the International Monetary and Financial Conference held at Bretton Woods, New Hampshire, in July 1944. In December 1945 the required number of countries had ratified the agreements, and in March 1946 the first meeting of the Board of Governors was held. The IMF commenced operations on March 1, 1947 at its headquarters in Washington DC.

International Security Standards: There are at present a number of security standards available for different financial applications. Most of them are internationally accepted and part of the ISO standards. These international standards such as the BS7799 have been accepted by the RBI. Banks, however, could also put in place measures which conform to their own policies and ensure regular and periodical audit.

The objectives of these standards are as listed below.

1. To provide management direction and support for information security which is a base prerequisite for BS7799.
2. To manage information security within the organisation,

maintain the security of organisational information processing facilities and information assets accessed by third parties, and to maintain the security of information when the responsibility for information processing has been outsourced to another organisation.

3. To maintain appropriate protection of corporate assets and ensure that information assets receive an appropriate level of protection.
4. To reduce risks of human error, theft, fraud or misuse of facilities and minimise the damage from security incidents and malfunctions and learn from such incidents.
5. To ensure the correct and secure operation of information processing facilities, minimise the risk of systems failures, to protect the integrity of software and information and maintain the integrity and availability of information processing and communication.
6. To control access to information, prevent unauthorised access, detect unauthorised activities and ensure information security when using mobile computing and tele-networking facilities.
7. To ensure security is built into operational systems, to prevent loss, modification or misuse of user data in application systems.
8. To counteract interruptions to business activities and critical business processes from the effects of major failures or disasters.
9. To prevent breaches of any criminal or civil law, statutory, regulatory or contractual obligations and of any security requirements, ensure compliance of systems with organisational security policies and standards and minimise interference to/from the system audit process.

International Swaps and Derivatives Association (ISDA): It promotes orderly practices in the swap market, conducts research on the volume and quality of transactions, and public understanding. ISDA, established in 1985, is a not-for-profit corporation, with headquarters in New York City. Its members include over 140 institutions worldwide representing dealers in swaps, corporations, software firms, and law firms. ISDA, formerly known as the International Swap Dealers Association, changed its name in August 1993.

Invoice Currency: It is the currency in which an invoice for exported or imported goods is denominated.

Involuntary Bankruptcy: See Bankruptcy, *16*.

Irrevocable Letter of Credit: See Letter of Credit, *141*.

Islamic Development Bank: It finances economic aid and social development in member countries. It also supports Muslim communities in non-member countries. Membership is open to all countries which are members of the Islamic Conference. It was established in 1973 with headquarters in Jeddah, Saudi Arabia.

Jj

Joint Account: An account owned by two or more persons. Either party can conduct transactions separately or together as set forth in the deposit account contract.

Joint Liability Group (JLG): A JLG is an informal group comprising of 5 to 10 individual members who come together for the purpose of availing bank loans either individually or through the group mechanism against a mutual guarantee.

Micro finance sector caters to the needs of poor people and the loans given by micro finance institutions are not backed by any security (i.e. unsecured loans). As is well-known, unsecured loans are always risky because very little can be done if loans are not repaid. To meet this challenge micro finance institutions have adopted the concept of JLGs.

In a JLG, the borrowers make a group among themselves and the micro finance institution gives loan to the group. A person in that group is appointed as leader of the group and each person is responsible for the loan taken by any member of the group. If any one person in the group defaults then other group members will have to pay for that.

The Group concept is helpful because everyone is monitored by others in the group and the borrower utilises his money properly. If any one defaults, other group members will make all possible efforts to take money back from him. This arrangement motivates the borrowers to maintain discipline while asking for loan and utilising it appropriately. It is possible that sometimes the group also defaults. However, it is a different problem which is less likely to occur. JLG concept helps the micro finance institutions to reduce the default risk. Moreover, it inculcates the habit of disciplined management of finance among the poor.

The National Bank for Agriculture and Rural Development (NABARD) is operating a joint liability group (JLG) scheme to provide access to institutional credit to small, marginal, tenant farmers, oral lessees and share croppers.

Joint Venture: A joint venture is a business or industrial organisation set up by two or more firms by combining their resources, management and skill. It may be formed with a limited objective of undertaking a project or research work. Alternatively, it can be a multinational involving co-operation among different domestic and foreign companies. Joint ventures are different from mergers in that they involve the creation of a new business firm rather than a joint effort of two or more existing companies.

A joint venture may be set up by individuals, corporations, governments, or some combination of these three. Following are the examples of a joint venture: (a) two large international oil companies jointly form a subsidiary to explore for oil in a region, (b) a multinational firm establishes a subsidiary with local partners in a developing country to manufacture and sell in that market, (c) a large manufacturing firm based in US forms a joint venture with a state-owned enterprise in India, and (d) two firms agree to develop a new technology by creating a joint research and development subsidiary.

Kk

Key Currency: It means currency which is used as an international reserve asset and also as means of financing international transactions. It is easily convertible into gold. Two notable key currencies are US dollar and British pound.

Key Currency Country: It refers to the country whose currency is used world-wide as a reserve asset as well as for undertaking trade transactions. US is one such country whose national currency, namely dollar is functioning as an international key currency. The advantage to US is that it is exempt from pressures of balance of payments deficit. It need not reduce its gold stock or its stock of foreign currency reserves as long as its foreign trading partners remain willing to accumulate balances in key currency (dollar) rather than to sell it in foreign exchange market. Thus, there will be no pressure on dollar to fall below its given exchange rate in response to the deficit.

Keynesian Economics: It refers to the economic ideas of British economist John Maynard Keynes (1883-1946) as propounded in his epoch-making book *The General Theory of Employment, Interest and Money* (1936) and other writings. Keynesian economics grew out of the turmoil caused by the Great Depression (q.v.) of early 1930s. Keynes believed that government intervention in a free enterprise economy was necessary to ensure sustained economic development. He maintained that insufficient aggregate demand causes unemployment and excessive demand results in inflation. Therefore, government should manipulate the level of aggregate demand by varying the level of its own expenditure and taxation. For example, to avoid a recession, the government should increase spending on public works, reduce taxes, and provide easy credit. These measures would lead to more investment, higher employment and increased private spending.

Keynes rejected outright the classical reasoning that working of price mechanism would always bring economic activities to a level of full employment. He believed that in the modern day economic life aggregate demand can be insufficient to absorb all the products that industry would produce if the factors of production were fully employed. If the continuity of the circular flow of money is broken, a tendency toward under-employment of labour and capital emerges with a correspondingly low level of national income.

Keynes developed a new theory which was concerned with certain economic aggregates. He stressed the relationship between total income, total consumption, total saving and investment, and total employment. As a result of his work, new tools of analysis were introduced into economics which are valid till date to a large extent.

Kisan Credit Cards (KCC): KCC is a pioneering credit delivery innovation—launched by NABARD in August 1998—for providing adequate and timely credit to farmers under single window, with flexible and simplified procedure, adopting whole farm approach, including the short-term credit, medium term and long term credit needs of the borrowers for agriculture and allied activities and a reasonable component for consumption needs. KCC scheme aims at providing crop loans to farmers in a flexible and cost-effective manner. The scheme is being implemented in all the States and Union Territories by all commercial banks, RRBs, state co-operative banks, central co-operative banks, and primary agricultural co-operative societies.

Beneficiaries covered under the KCC are issued with a credit card and a pass book or a credit card-cum-pass book incorporating the name, address and particulars of land, borrowing limit, and the validity period. The introduction of KCCs was a significant innovation in the rural credit delivery mechanism. However, the outreach of the KCCs to cover all eligible farmers under the scheme has been hampered by the lack of updated land records, small landholdings and illiteracy of borrowers.

Kyoto Convention: The International Convention on the simplification and harmonization of Customs procedures (Kyoto Convention) was signed at Kyoto in May 1973 and entered into force in 1974. The Convention discussed the universal harmonisation of customs procedures, other than classification and valuation. The World Customs Organization (WCO) adopted the revised Convention in June 1999 reflecting current and expected future demands of international trade.

Ll

Late Charge: The fee charged for delinquent payment on an instalment loan, usually expressed as a percentage of the loan balance or payment. Also, a penalty imposed by a card issuer against a cardholder's account for failing to make minimum payments.

Lease: A contract transferring the use of property or occupancy of land, space, structures, or equipment in consideration of a payment (e.g. rent).

Lender: An individual or financial institution that lends money with the expectation that the money will be returned with interest.

Letter of Credit: It is a financial document issued by a bank at the request of the consignee guaranteeing payment to the shipper for cargo if certain terms and conditions are fulfilled. Normally, it contains a brief description of the goods, documents required, a shipping date, and an expiration date after which payment will no longer be made.

Irrevocable Letter of Credit is one which obligates the issuing bank to pay the exporter when all terms and conditions of the letter of credit have been met. None of the terms and conditions may be changed without the consent of all parties to the letter of credit.

Revocable Letter of Credit is subject to possible recall or amendment at the option of the applicant, without the approval of the beneficiary.

Confirmed Letter of Credit is issued by a foreign bank with its validity confirmed by a U.S. bank. An exporter who requires a confirmed letter of credit from the buyer is assured payment from the US bank in case the foreign buyer or bank defaults.

Documentary Letter of Credit is one for which the issuing bank stipulates that certain documents must accompany a draft. The documents assure the applicant (importer) that the merchandise has been shipped and that title to the goods has been transferred to the importer.

Liabilities of a Bank: See Commercial Bank, *37*.

Liberalised Exchange Rate Management System (LERMS): On March 1, 1992, partial convertibility of the rupee was introduced in India in the form of a dual exchange rate system called the LERMS along with other measures of liberalisation in the areas of trade, industry, foreign investment and the import of gold. Under the system all foreign exchange receipts on current account transactions (exports, remittances, *etc*.) were required to be surrendered to the authorised dealers (ADs) in full. The rate of exchange for conversion of 60 percent of the proceeds of these transactions was the market rate quoted by the ADs while the remaining 40 percent of the proceeds were converted at the RBI's official rate. The ADs in turn were to surrender to the RBI 40 percent of their purchase of foreign currencies representing current receipts at the official rate of exchange announced by the RBI. They were free to retain the balance of 60 percent of foreign exchange for being sold in the free market for permissible transactions.

Deficiencies of LERMS: As a transitional arrangement, LERMS served to impart stability to the external value of the rupee and to prepare the narrow inter-bank foreign exchange market for an increased volume of transactions. However, it involved a dual exchange rate system, implicit in which was a tax on exports arising out of the differential in the rates of surrender of export proceeds. Moreover, the system could not be sustained for long as it called for the rationing of subsidised foreign exchange among certain imports, inevitably resulting in distortions in resource allocation. As it functioned, there were indications of the diversion of remittances from their normal route to the capital account, since inflows into certain non-resident rupee deposit accounts were allowed full conversion at the market exchange rate whereas remittances in the form of current transfers were to be converted at the market exchange rate only to the extent of 60 percent. The system was modified when a downward adjustment in the official exchange rate took place in early December 1992 and ultimate convergence of the dual rates was made effective from March 1, 1993.

Modified LERMS: Some of the features of the so-called modified LERMS were as follows.

1. All foreign exchange receipts were converted at market determined rates of exchange from March 2, 1993.
2. The unification of exchange rates marked an important step in the progress towards convertibility on the current account. The freely floating exchange rate regime continued to operate within the framework of exchange control. Current receipts were surrendered to the banking system, which in turn met the demand for foreign exchange arising out of permissible purposes. The rates of exchange at which these transactions were effected were determined in the market.
3. The ADs were not required to surrender to the RBI any part of foreign exchange sold to them. The RBI could, however, at its discretion, enter the market to purchase/sell foreign exchange. The RBI's obligation to sell forex for any purpose other than debt service payments of the Government of India was replaced. It currently buys/sells only US dollars, which in March 1993 replaced, the Pound Sterling as the intervention currency. From March 2002, Euro became an additional intervention currency.
4. With effect from October 4, 1995, the RBI discontinued quoting its buying and selling rate. At present, the RBI announces a reference rate based on the quotations of a few select banks in Mumbai at twelve noon every day. Among other things, the reference rate is also applicable to special drawing rights transactions.
5. In order to ensure that exchange rate of the rupee fully reflected the demand-supply situation and in furtherance of the move towards eliminating transaction through reserves, it was decided with effect from July 3, 1995 to route debt service payment

(civil) of Government of India through the market.

LIC: See Life Insurance Corporation of India, *144*.

Lien: Legal claim against a property. Once the property is sold, the lien holder is then paid the amount that is owed.

Life Insurance Corporation of India (LIC): It was established in 1956 when the life insurance business was nationalised in India.

Line of Credit: A pre-approved loan authorization with a specific borrowing limit based on creditworthiness. A line of credit allows borrowers to obtain a number of loans without re-applying each time as long as the total of borrowed funds does not exceed the credit limit.

Liquidity of an Asset: Liquidity of an asset means how easily it can be converted into cash and at what loss of its capital value. If an asset cannot be converted into cash easily (i.e. at short notice) or at minimum loss of its value, it is less liquid.

Liquidity, International: It is the aggregate stock of assets such as gold, foreign exchange and special drawing rights (SDRs) held by the national monetary authority and which is available unconditionally to settle the country's imbalance in international transactions. A country's reserve position in the International Monetary Fund (q.v.) is also included herein as it is available for use by the country concerned in the case of balance of payments deficit. The amount of liquidity needed depends on the size and duration of the deficit. The term may be used to refer to the reserves of an individual country or to the sum of reserves of all countries.

Loan Contract: The written agreement between a borrower and a lender in which the terms and conditions of the loan are set.

Loan Proceeds: The net amount of funds that a lending

institution disburses under the terms of a loan, and which the borrower then owes.

Local Cheque: A cheque payable by, at, or through a bank in the same cheque processing region as the location of the branch of the depository bank. The depository bank is the bank into which the cheque was deposited.

***Lok Adalats* (Peoples Courts):** In the area of dispute settlement, the Legal Services Authority Act, 1987 has conferred statutory basis on the *Lok Adalats*. The RBI issued guidelines to commercial banks and financial institutions to enable them to make increasing use of the forum of *Lok Adalats*. In terms of the guidelines, banks could settle banking disputes involving an amount up to ₹ 5 lakh through the forum of *Lok Adalats*. The Central Government, in consultation with the RBI, decided to increase the monetary ceiling of cases to be referred to the *Lok Adalats* organised by Civil Courts. Accordingly, on August 3, 2004, the RBI enhanced the monetary ceiling of cases to be referred to *Lok Adalats* organised by civil courts to ₹ 20 lakh as against the earlier ceiling of ₹ 5 lakh.

London Interbank Offered Rate (LIBOR): Often used as a basis for pricing Euroloans. LIBOR represents the interest rate at which first class banks in London are prepared to offer dollar deposits to other first class banks. There are a number of similar rates like Hong Kong Inter-bank Offer Rate (HIBOR); Singapore Inter-bank Offer Rate (SIBOR); Toronto Inter-bank Offer Rate (TIBOR); and Mumbai Inter-bank Bid and Offer Rates (MIBOR).

Loss Carry Back: It is a legal provision permitting business assessees to use the operating losses of one year to offset profits of preceding years. Since a business which suffers a loss after having paid taxes in prior years can claim a tax refund after losses appear, such provisions reduce the tax-created risks of business. The time period for which losses can be so carried back is specified in the tax law. See also Loss Carry Forward.

Loss Carry Forward: It refers to a legal provision permitting business assessees to use losses of one year to offset profits of succeeding years. Under a system of income tax based on net principle, losses of income should attract same considerations as gains. In other words, net gains should attract tax while net losses should be considered for negative tax, i.e. a government refund. In practice, governments do not go so far to help loss-making units but they do provide facilities for carry forward of losses. Loss carry forward (vertical compensation) against future profits amounts to a refund but the taxpayer has to wait for it and this waiting involves loss in terms of interest foregone.

Facility for loss carry forward reduces tax-created risks of business and investment, mitigates disincentive effects of fluctuating incomes, and thereby promotes private enterprise. It can be regarded as a proxy for income averaging provisions.

Loss carry forward is a common feature of income tax systems the world over though the number of years allowed for the carry forward differ from system to system. See also Loss Carry Back.

Loss Set Off: It is a legal provision allowing counterbalancing of losses in one category of activity against profits of another kind of activity within the same taxable year. In the income tax laws of most countries, income chargeable to tax is computed under different heads. The aggregation of gross total income is relatively easy if income under each head and from each source is positive. However, loss may be sustained in one or more sources under one or more heads of income. Therefore, in the computation of gross total income of an assessee, appropriate adjustments are made of the losses suffered by him. Such adjustments are made in two ways: (a) inter-source adjustment in the same assessment year, and (b) inter-head adjustment in the same assessment year. Provisions of (b) are applied only if a loss cannot be set off, fully or partly, under (a).

Loss set off (horizontal compensation) is a common feature of income tax systems the world over though the conditions for it differ from system to system.

Lump Sum Tax: It refers to taxation of income, net wealth etc. expressed as a certain fixed sum rather than calculated under the ordinary tax law. This method is used for administrative convenience where facts are difficult to establish. In a lump sum tax, an individual cannot take action to alter his tax liability.

Mm

Managed Float: Managed float (also called dirty float) refers to floating exchange rate system in which government intervention takes place secretly. Overtly, the government maintains that it is the demand and supply forces which determine exchange rate but secretly it may ask the central bank to intervene in the exchange market to stabilise the currency at the desired level. International Monetary Fund has developed some guidelines for such interventions, and named this system as managed float. It is a device to correct disequilibrium in the balance of payments. See also Clean Float.

Market Capitalisation: It is the value of a company calculated by multiplying the price of its shares on the stock exchange by the number of shares issued.

Market Economy: The national economy of a country that relies on market forces to determine levels of production, consumption, investment, and savings without government intervention.

MAT: See Minimum Alternative Tax, *152*.

Matching Grant: It is a subsidy that is conditional on a co-payment or contribution by an industry or enterprise.

Maturity: The date on which the principal balance of a loan, bond, or other financial instrument becomes due and payable.

Merchant Bank: It is a financial institution which performs a wide range of activities including advising companies on take-overs, amalgamations, flotations and share issues.

Micro Credit: See Micro Finance, *149*.

Micro Finance: Micro finance is the provision of a diverse range of financial services and products including small loans (micro credit), savings accounts, insurance, pensions and money transfers. These are designed to assist people living in poverty who are not able to access financial services in the mainstream banking sector because they have no collateral, formal identification or steady income.

The proposed Micro Finance Services Regulation Bill defines micro finance services as providing financial assistance to an individual or an eligible client, either directly or through a group mechanism for an amount, not exceeding ₹ 50,000 in aggregate (₹ 1,50,000 if for housing purposes).

Salient Features of Micro Finance: These are as under:

1. Borrowers are from the low-income group.
2. Loans are of small amount.
3. Loans are for short duration.
4. Loans are offered without collaterals.
5. Loans are generally given for income generation purpose.
6. Repayment frequency is high.
7. Loan terms vary, but once repaid, the money is recycled and lent out to someone else.

Micro Finance and Micro Credit Distinguished: Micro finance is different from micro credit. Micro finance is a broad category of services, which includes micro credit. Micro credit is provision of credit services to poor clients. Micro credit is one of the aspects of micro finance and the two are often confused. Under micro credit, small amounts of loans are given to the borrower but under micro finance besides loans many other financial services are provided such as savings account, insurance etc. Therefore micro finance is a wider concept as compared to micro credit.

Micro credit is the provision of small, collateral-free loans to people living in poverty to use as business capital. Loans are used to start or grow micro enterprises that help give them a regular income—whether it is a small farm, food stall, jewellery-making business or taxi. They may use loans to buy stock or equipment, creating a sustainable livelihood for themselves and their families. Through the profits they earn, they are able to provide for their children and repay the loans over time.

Micro Finance and Allied Services: Apart from providing small loans, micro finance also includes a range of financial services to the poor. Some of these are as follows:

Savings Accounts: These are meant to help provide a safety net in times of need and help to plan for the future. Without an alternative, people living in poverty hide their money in boxes under their beds or in holes in the ground. They also put their money into assets—such as livestock or pieces of jewellery, which offer little real security—they can be stolen, deteriorate or be destroyed by natural disasters.

Micro savings are deposit services offered by financial institutions that allow people living in poverty to securely store small amounts of money. Micro finance institutions offer savings facilities—some even make them compulsory, encouraging families to plan for unexpected expenses so they can have the freedom to invest in healthcare, education, housing and their businesses when the need arises.

In many cases, banking regulations do not allow micro finance institutions to directly offer micro savings services. Agency arrangements with banks can help overcome this problem.

Micro Insurance: This is meant to protect against emergencies and disasters. Micro insurance is insurance for low-income households that protects against unforeseen events so that savings and working capital can be maintained rather than eroded. Like savings, it helps provide security against the many risks faced by those living in poverty.

Innovative products offered by micro finance institutions cover policyholders with crop, loan, health, life and property insurance—offering families a safety net when an unexpected hardship occurs so they are not forced back into poverty.

Micro Pensions: Micro pensions are accumulation superannuation accounts. They are funded by an individual's contribution and, in some cases, a matched contribution from the government. They are meant to help provide an income in old age.

Fund Transfers and Remittance Products: These are meant to help families, living far apart, access their incomes. Money transfers are domestic and international electronic transfers of money. They are used for a variety of purposes, including regular bill payment, one-time-only money needs, delivering money from people working in urban areas to their family members in rural areas, and sending money from migrants to family members in their country of origin (remittances).

Many developing countries lack any viable money transfer services, and substantial volumes of global remittances continue to flow through informal and sometimes dangerous underground channels which are outside government supervision and regulation. Micro finance institutions are increasingly trying to seek alliances with banks and money transfer companies to offer safe, convenient and lower-cost transfers to their clients, many utilising mobile phone technologies.

Micro Finance Clients and Activities: Often, people do not have enough money when they face a need, so they borrow. A poor family might borrow from relatives to buy land, from a moneylender to buy rice, or from a micro finance institution to buy a sewing machine.

In urban areas, micro finance activities are diverse and include shopkeepers, service providers, artisans, street vendors, manufacturers and so on. In rural areas, they are typically small-scale farmers and others who are engaged in small income-generating activities such as food processing and trade.

Micro finance institutions (MFIs) have clients that run businesses such as convenience stores, bakeries, canteens, fruit and vegetable stalls or recycling shops. Others offer services in carpentry, transport, tailoring, food manufacturing or repairs, while many rural clients have small farms where they keep animals or produce crops such as rice.

A major incentive for clients to repay loans is their ability to secure subsequent, larger loans once initial loans are repaid. This enables entrepreneurs to grow their businesses more and more with each subsequent loan, increasing their productivity, income and the living standards of their family.

Borrowers often form guaranteeing groups, particularly in early loan cycles. This community approach provides support when an individual is unable to make a loan repayment, possibly due to illness or other hardship.

Businesses of clients are vulnerable to a range of factors. In most cases, MFIs provide information and basic business training to equip clients with the knowledge and skills they need to make the most of their loan.

People can use small loans to start businesses such as the following: tailoring shops, vegetable farms, small grocery stores, hairdressing saloons, bicycle repair shops, tea shops, pig breeding farms, basket weaving, rickshaw taxi services, clothing market stalls, fishing operations, construction businesses etc.

Micro Insurance: See Micro Finance, *149*.

Micro Pensions: See Micro Finance, *149*.

Minimum Alternative Tax (MAT): Income tax laws throughout the world generally provide for a number of tax concessions. A clever profit-making company may arrange its affairs in such a manner that the cumulative effect of all tax concessions is to reduce its income declared in the tax return to zero. MAT is a device to keep a Zero Tax Company (q.v.) within the tax net.

In India, if the income disclosed by a company in the tax return (after claiming all deductions) is less than 30 percent of its book profits then this 30 percent of the book profits is subject to tax. The concept of minimum alternative tax also prevails in the US where it is called Alternative Minimum Tax (AMT). However, under its laws if in the subsequent years the company pays tax on its regular income (income declared in the tax return) then the minimum alternative tax paid earlier on its adjusted taxable income is allowed as a set off against the tax payable on regular income. In the US, AMT was designed as a part of the

Tax Reform Act of 1986, in response to the concern that a number of firms that reported positive book profits paid no corporate tax to the Federal Government.

Minimum Balance: The amount of money required to be on deposit in an account to qualify the depositor for special services or to waive a service charge.

Missing Payment: A payment that has been made but not credited to the appropriate account.

Mixed Economy: An economic system in which both the government and private enterprise play important roles with regard to production, consumption, investment, and savings.

Monetary Gold: Gold held by monetary authorities (central banks) as part of a country's official reserves. See also Non-monetary Gold.

Monetary Policy: Monetary policy refers to the expansion or contraction of money and credit supply in an economy. Since monetary policy includes the regulation of both the volume and allocation of credit therefore credit policy is a part of the overall monetary policy. Monetary policy operates through changes in the stock of money and changes in the cost and availability of credit. The operation of monetary policy rests on the interrelationship between the stock of money, output and prices. Through money creation, credit is made available to productive enterprises. The availability of credit has favourable impact on output. Simultaneously, increase in money supply raises demand, exerting pressure on prices. The output effect and the price effect must be considered together to assess the overall effect of a monetary measure on the economy.

Objectives of Monetary Policy: Monetary policy is of crucial importance in the context of the overall development of a country. The objectives of monetary policy are, by and large, the same as those of general economic policy.

Price stability is of prime concern for a developing country like India. The term price stability is not used here in a rigid sense to mean price fixity. A modest increase of 2 to 3 percent in price level per annum is compatible, sometimes even desirable, with the general connotation of price stability. Since price rise is closely linked with the supply of money therefore monetary policy holds the key to price stability. This is why the economists stress growth with stability as the ideal objective of economic policy of a country.

Many developing countries suffer from chronic deficits in their trade balances. This is so because their imports exceed exports. Since imports are essential for the development of the economy therefore it is necessary to increase exports to pay for imports. Domestic price stability is a precondition for increasing exports. Monetary policy becomes relevant in this connection.

Rapid economic development is another concern of policymakers in developing countries. All policies of the Government, including the monetary policy, are geared to achieve this objective. The need for monetary resources is linked with the increase in output and the desire for investment. Monetary policy should react to such changes in time and adequately. It should ensure proper balance between the monetary needs of the economy and money supply. Monetary policy, by influencing the cost, volume and direction of credit, contributes to the achievement of general objectives of economic policy.

Monetary Policy and Fiscal Policy Interface: Monetary policy and Fiscal Policy (q.v.) are two important instruments of the general economic policy of a government. Monetary policy and fiscal policy affect the economy in different ways. Fiscal policy is more direct in its effects. It straightway determines government expenditure and affects private expenditure through taxation measures. Fiscal policy, through budgetary deficits or surpluses, determines changes in government debt and hence issue of new currency. Contrarily, monetary policy has no direct spending and income effects. The effects of monetary policy are indirect and depend on the reactions of lenders and borrowers to the changes brought about by monetary policy. Changes in the monetary policy are more frequent and can be made at any time during a year. However, changes in fiscal policy are less frequent and may require parliamentary approval. See also Fiscal Policy.

Money: Under a system of simple commodity production, exchange of goods was accomplished largely through barter. The main difficulty of the barter system was the double coincidence of wants. In a modern economy, characterised by acute specialisation and exchange, barter system would just be impossible. It is, therefore, necessary to accept some one thing as a medium of exchange. Any generally accepted thing which serves as a medium of exchange may be called money. Historically, a variety of things have served as money including goats, coins, paper currency and demand deposits of banks.

Kinds of Money: Money may be in the form of some commodity (goat, silver etc.) or merely a nominal unit of account like paper money. These days three kinds of money is important, viz. coins, paper currency and bank deposit money. Coins are example of metallic money. Their intrinsic value is less than their face value and therefore they are not full-bodied but only token money.

In modern times, paper currency has replaced metallic money. Paper money is accepted by the people readily in all kinds of transactions. This is so because government makes it legal tender. In other words, it circulates by command (fiat) and therefore is called *fiat money*. Deposit money denotes bank deposits against which cheques can be drawn. Normally, demand deposits are taken into account for this purpose. Deposit money is not a legal tender like currency notes. Because it circulates by trust commanded by its issuers therefore it is often called *fiduciary money*

Functions of Money: The first and the most important function of money is to act as a medium of exchange. As a matter of fact, money is defined in terms of this unique function. Other functions of money are more or less derived from this function. By using money as a medium of exchange, a society can get rid of the difficulties of barter system. By the use of money, exchange becomes easy and this promotes specialisation which has its own advantages in a modern society.

Money serves as a unit of account or standard of value. Money is used to express and compare the values of goods and services which enter the market. Values of goods and services when expressed in terms of money are called prices. With the help of these prices, the ratio of exchange between any two commodities can easily be determined. As a measure of value, money helps us to know almost instantly how much sugar is worth how much butter.

Unfortunately, money as a standard of value is not fixed but a variable one. This is so because the value of money, i.e. the purchasing power of money itself changes from time to time in view of the changes in the general level of prices. The same ten rupee note purchases different quantities of sugar at different times. It is like measuring cloth with a rubber meter the length of which varies with stretching efforts. This instability in money as a standard of value can cause great turmoil in the economy. It is interesting to note that in measuring weight, length and time man has devised invariable units, namely kilogram, metre and minute which are fixed over time and across regions. However, a fixed measure of value is yet to be achieved.

Money serves as a measure of deferred or future payments. These deferred payments pertain to debts and interest thereon, insurance premiums and future instalments of goods purchased at present. The agreements of deferred payments are in terms of money the value of which is subject to fluctuations. Therefore, money is an imperfect standard of deferred payments also. This attribute has serious repercussions for debtors and creditors.

Money also serves as a store of value. People find it easy to hold some of their wealth in money form rather than in terms of commodities. Value can, of course, be stored in terms of other assets but they are not as readily acceptable means of payment as money. However, variations in the value of money cause disturbances in its role as a store of value as in the case of its function as a measure of value and as a standard of deferred payments. See also Electronic Money (E-Money).

Money Illusion: It arises when a person associates money directly with its face value without considering its purchasing power. If wages of a worker are doubled when prices double, his real wages remain constant. However, if the worker feels better off after the wage hike, he suffers from money illusion. See also Veil of Money.

Money Market: Money market is the most important segment of the financial system as it provides the fulcrum for equilibrating short-term demand for and supply of funds, thereby facilitating the conduct of monetary policy. It is a market for short-term funds with a maturity of up to one year and includes financial instruments that are close substitutes for money. The main instruments comprising the money market are: (a) call money/notice money, (b) certificates of deposit (CDs), (c) treasury bills (abolished with effect from April 1997), (d) repurchase agreements (repos), (e) commercial bills, (f) commercial paper (CPs), and (g) inter-corporate funds.

While inter-bank money markets and central bank lending via repo operations or discounting, provide liquidity for banks, private non-bank money market instruments, such as commercial bills and commercial paper provide liquidity to the commercial sector. Unlike in developed economies where money markets are promoted by financial intermediaries out of efficiency considerations, in India, as in many other developing countries, the evolution of the money market and its structure has been integrated into the overall deregulation process of the financial sector.

The money market is generally expected to perform three broad functions.

1. It provides an equilibrating mechanism to even out demand

for and supply of short-term funds.

2. It also presents a focal point for central bank intervention for influencing liquidity and general level of interest rates in the economy.
3. It provides reasonable access to providers and users of short-term funds to fulfil their borrowing and investment requirements at an efficient market clearing price.

The RBI is the most important constituent of the money market. Owing to its implications for conducting monetary policy, the money market falls under the direct purview of regulation of the RBI. The primary objective of the RBI's operations in the money market has been to ensure that short-term interest rates and liquidity are maintained at levels which are consistent with the overall monetary policy objectives, *viz.* maintaining price stability, ensuring adequate flow of credit to the productive sectors of the economy and maintaining orderly conditions in the financial markets. Liquidity and interest rates in the system are influenced by the RBI through the use of various instruments at its disposal which, *inter alia*, include the following.

1. Variations in cash reserve ratio.
2. Standing facilities/refinance schemes.
3. Repo and reverse repo transactions.
4. Changes in the bank rate.
5. Open market operations.
6. Foreign exchange swap operations.

Recognising the important role of the market in the monetary policy process, the RBI has taken active interest in continuously refining the money market instruments in order to have greater control over the liquidity in the system and for creating an efficient mechanism to impart interest rate signals.

Money Supply: The amount of money (coins, paper currency, and bank deposits) that is in circulation in the economy.

Mortgage: A debt instrument used in a real estate transaction where the property is the collateral for the loan. A mortgage gives the lender a right to take possession of the property if the borrower fails to pay off the loan.

Mortgage Loan: A loan made by a lender to a borrower for the financing of real property.

Mortgagee: The lender in a mortgage loan relationship.

Mortgagor: The borrower in a mortgage loan relationship.

Multilateral Aid: See Foreign Aid, *95*.

Multinational Corporation: A multinational corporation (MNC) or transnational corporation is a large sized, dominant company involved in production and trade of a wide range of commodities or services and based in two or more countries. It consists of a parent company from where it emerged and where its ownership and management rest. In other countries, there are subsidiaries which are partly owned and managed by people of various nationalities. Large capital base, technological superiority, innovations, advertisements and an oligopolistic ownership have led to the growth of transnational corporation since the early 1960s.

Mutual Funds: Mutual funds are very popular all over the world and they play an important role in the financial system of many countries. Mutual funds are an ideal medium for investment by small investors in the stock market. Mutual funds pool together the investments of small investors for participation in the stock market. Being institutional investors, mutual funds can afford market analysis generally not available to individual investors. Furthermore, mutual funds can diversify the portfolio in a better way as compared with individual investors due to the expertise and availability of funds.

Mutual funds are an ideal vehicle for investment by retail investors in the stock market for several reasons. First, it pools the investments of small investors together, increasing thereby the participation in the stock market. Secondly, mutual funds, being institutional investors, can afford market analysis by experts generally not available or accessible to individual investors, providing thereby informed decisions to the small investors. Thirdly, mutual funds can diversify the portfolio in a better way as compared with individual investors due to the expertise and availability of funds.

Nn

National Bank for Agriculture and Rural Development (NABARD): Set up in 1982, NABARD is the apex institution accredited with all matters concerning policy, planning and operations in the field of credit for agriculture and other economic activities in rural areas in India. NABARD serves as an apex refinancing agency for the institutions providing investment and production credit in rural areas.

Other main activities of NABARD include: (a) initiating measures towards institution building for improving absorptive capacity of the credit delivery system, including monitoring, formulation of rehabilitation schemes, restructuring of credit institutions and training of personnel, (b) co-ordinating the rural financing activities of all institutions engaged in developmental work at the field level, (c) maintaining liaison with the Government of India, the State Governments, the RBI and other national level institutions concerned with policy formulation, and (d) undertaking monitoring and evaluation of projects refinanced by it.

National Electronic Funds Transfer (NEFT): The NEFT was launched by the RBI in November 2005 as a more secure, nation-wide retail electronic payment system to facilitate funds transfer by the bank customers, between the networked bank branches in the country. It has, however, been observed that the public sector banks are not the most active users of this product and the majority of NEFT outward transactions are originated by a few new-generation private sector banks and foreign banks.

In order to popularise the e-payments in the country, the RBI, on its part, waived the service charges to be levied on the member banks, till March 31, 2009, in respect of the Real Time Gross Settlement (RTGS) and NEFT transactions. The RBI also provides, free of charge, intra-day liquidity to the banks for the RTGS transactions. The service charges to be levied by banks from their customers for RTGS and NEFT have, however, been deregulated and left to the discretion of the individual banks. While some of the banks have rationalised their service charges and a few have made it even cost-free to the customers, there are also certain banks that have fixed unreasonably high service charges for providing these services to their customers—even though the RBI provides these services to the banks free of charge.

National Housing Bank (NHB): Established in 1988, it is the chief refinance institution in the housing sector. In recognition of the need for developing a network of specialised housing finance institutions in the country, the National Housing Bank was set up in July, 1988 as a wholly owned subsidiary of the RBI under the National Housing Bank Act, 1987, to function as an apex bank for the housing finance. NHB regulates HFCs, refinances their operations and expands the spread of housing finance to different income groups all over the country, while functioning within the overall framework of the housing policy. It has also helped in diverting increasing proportions of annual provident fund accumulations for housing finance through housing linked savings schemes for provident fund subscribers.

National Stock Exchange of India Limited (NSE): It is located in Mumbai, India. NSE was established in the mid-1990s as a demutualised electronic exchange. NSE provides a modern, fully automated screen-based trading system, with over two lakh trading terminals, through which investors in every nook and corner of India can trade. NSE has played a critical role in reforming the Indian securities market and in bringing unparalleled transparency, efficiency and market integrity.

Though a number of other exchanges exist, NSE and the Bombay Stock Exchange (BSE) are the two most significant stock exchanges in India, and between them are responsible for the vast majority of share transactions. NSE's flagship index, the CNX NIFTY 50, is used extensively by investors in India and around the world to take exposure to the Indian equities market.

NSE was started by a clutch of leading Indian financial

institutions. It offers trading, clearing and settlement services in equity, debt and equity derivatives. It is India's largest exchange, globally in cash market trades, in currency trading and index options. NSE has diversified shareholding. There are many domestic and global institutions and companies that hold stake in the exchange.

NSC was incorporated in 1992 and recognised as a stock exchange in 1993, at a time when P.V. Narasimha Rao was the Prime Minister of India and Dr. Manmohan Singh was the Finance Minister. It was set up to bring in transparency in the markets. Promoted by leading financial institutions, essentially led by IDBI at the behest of the Government of India, it was incorporated in November 1992 as a tax-paying company. In April 1993, it was recognised as a stock exchange under the Securities Contracts (Regulation) Act, 1956. NSE commenced operations in the Wholesale Debt Market (WDM) segment in June 1994. The Capital market (Equities) segment of the NSE commenced operations in November 1994, while operations in the Derivatives segment commenced in June 2000.

NSE changed the way the Indian markets functioned, in the early 1990s, by replacing floor-based trading with nationwide screen-based electronic trading, which took trading to the doorstep of the investor. The exchange was mainly set up to bring in transparency in the markets. Instead of trading membership being confined to a group of brokers, the NSE ensured that anyone who was qualified, experienced and met minimum financial requirements was allowed to trade.

In this context, the NSE was ahead of its times, when it separated ownership and management in the exchange under SEBI's supervision. The price information which could earlier be accessed only by a handful of people can now be seen by a client in a remote location with the same ease. The paper-based settlement has been replaced by electronic depository-based accounts and settlement of trades. A robust risk management system is in place, so that settlement guarantees could protect investors against broker defaults.

NSE was also instrumental in creating the National Securities Depository Limited (NSDL) which allows investors to securely hold and transfer their shares and bonds electronically. It also allows investors to hold and trade in as few as one share or bond. This not only makes holding financial instruments convenient, but more importantly eliminates the need for paper certificates and greatly reduces the incidents of forged or fake certificates and fraudulent transactions that had plagued the Indian stock market. NSDL's security, combined with the transparency, lower transaction prices and efficiency that the NSE offers, has greatly increased the attractiveness of the Indian stock market to domestic and international investors.

Negotiation Credit: It is a letter given by a bank advising a manufacturer or seller that the bank is authorized to accept and negotiate drafts drawn on a specified customer without liability on the part of the bank, usually for a stated amount and liable to withdrawal at any time.

Net Worth: It is the value of a business attributable to the ordinary shareholders. This value comprises the total assets of the business less liabilities to all those other than ordinary shareholders.

No Frills Account: See Financial Exclusion and Financial Inclusion, *86*.

Non-banking Financial Companies (NBFCs): In the multi-tier financial system of India, NBFCs stand apart for more than one reason. Though these companies essentially do the job of financial intermediation, they are still not fully comparable with the other segments of the financial system. This is so in view of the wide variations in the profile of the players in this sector in terms of their nature of activity—lending, investment, lease, hire purchase, chit fund, pure deposit mobilisation, fee based activity etc.—the volume of activity, the sources of funding they rely on (public deposits and non-public deposits), method of raising resources, deployment pattern etc. This has naturally resulted in the creation of multifarious categories of NBFCs and therefore, diverse regulatory dispensation by RBI.

Classification of NBFCs: NBFCs comprise a heterogeneous lot of privately-owned, small-sized financial intermediaries which provide a variety of services including equipment leasing, hire purchase, loans, investments and chit fund activities. These companies play an important role in providing credit to the unorganised sector and to the small borrowers at the local level. Hire purchase finance is by far the largest activity of NBFCs.

Though heterogeneous, NBFCs can be broadly classified into three categories: (a) asset finance companies (such as equipment leasing and hire purchase), (b) loan companies, and (c) investment companies.

A separate category of NBFCs, called the residuary non-banking companies (RNBCs), also exists as it has not been categorised into any one of the above referred three categories.

Besides, there are miscellaneous non-banking companies (chit funds), mutual benefit financial companies (*Nidhis* and unnotified *Nidhis*) and housing finance companies.

In terms of regulation and supervision, there are two broad categories of Non-banking Financial Companies (NBFCs), viz. Non-banking Financial Companies–Deposit Taking (NBFCs-D) and Non-banking Financial Companies–Non-deposit Taking (NBFCs-ND). While NBFCs-D have been regulated by the RBI from 1963, an amendment to the RBI Act in 1997 empowered the RBI to regulate and supervise all categories of NBFCs more comprehensively. NBFCs-ND, until recently, were subject to minimal regulation as they were non-deposit taking. Recognising, however, the growing importance of this segment and their linkages to banks and other financial institutions, capital adequacy and exposure norms were made applicable to NBFCs-ND with assets above ₹ 100 crore from April 1, 2007.

The role of NBFCs in transferring the funds from lenders to borrowers has been well-recognized. The main advantages of these companies are as under:

1. Customer orientation and prompt provision of services.
2. Concentration in the main financial centres.
3. Attractive rates of return offered.
4. Lower transactions costs of operations.
5. Quick decision-making ability.
6. Simplified sanction procedures.
7. Flexibility and timeliness in meeting the credit needs of specified sectors (like equipment leasing and hire purchase).

On account of these advantages, NBFCs have in recent years grown sizeably both in terms of their numbers as well as the volume of business transactions.

NBFCs have been the subject of focussed attention since the early 1990s. The rapid growth of NBFCs has led to a gradual blurring of dividing lines between banks and NBFCs, with the exception of the exclusive privilege that commercial banks exercise in the issuance of cheques.

NBFCs are widely dispersed across the country and their management exhibits varied degrees of professionalism. Furthermore, the depositors have varied degrees of perceptions regarding safety of their deposits while making an investment decision.

In June 2000, NBFCs registered with the RBI were permitted, with prior approval of the RBI, to set up insurance joint ventures for undertaking insurance business with risk participation. Similarly, NBFCs registered with the RBI that have net owned funds of ₹ 5 crore and more are permitted to undertake insurance business as agent of insurance companies on a fee basis, without any risk participation. A minimum 12 percent capital adequacy for NBFCs which want to enter into insurance joint ventures has been prescribed. If the company holds public deposits, the minimum capital adequacy has been proposed at 15 percent. Further, minimum net worth requirement of ₹ 500 crore, three years of continuous net profit, and maximum non-performing assets of 5 percent of the total outstanding leased/hire purchase assets and advances have been prescribed for NBFCs.

In February 2004, it was decided to allow NBFCs registered with the RBI to take up insurance agency business on a fee basis and without risk participation, without the approval of the RBI subject to certain conditions.

Non-financial Assets: These are tangible and intangible assets that are not financial assets.

Non-monetary Gold: Gold that is traded like any other commodity. Non-monetary gold is regarded as a commodity, rather than as a financial item, as its worth is principally derived from either its gold content or its value as a collector's piece. See also Monetary Gold.

Nostro Account: Account of a bank in a foreign bank is called nostro account. For example, a Mumbai bank's dollar account in a New York bank is a nostro account. See also Vostro Account.

Oo

Ocean Bill of Lading: See Bill of Lading, *22*.

Official Cheque: A cheque drawn on a bank and signed by an authorized bank official (also known as a cashier's cheque).

Official Development Assistance (ODA): It means economic or technical assistance extended to developing countries by the governments of developed countries and by international organizations, as contrasted with loans and investments financed by the private sector. ODA is construed as including only concessional transfers to developing countries, meaning that all or part of each ODA transaction is a grant or loan at rate of interest and/or on repayment terms more beneficial to the recipient than market rates and terms.

Official Rate: It is that rate of exchange which is approved and maintained by the government and at which official transactions and movements of currency take place.

Offset, Right of: Banks' legal right to seize funds that a guarantor or debtor may have on deposit to cover a loan in default. It is also known as right of setoff

On Board Bill of Lading: See Bill of Lading, *22*.

Online Banking: A service that allows an account holder to obtain account information and manage certain banking transactions through a personal computer via the financial institution's web site on the internet.

Open Market Operations: See Reserve Bank of India, *191*.

Open-end Credit: A credit agreement (typically a credit card) that allows a customer to borrow against a pre-approved credit line when purchasing goods and services. The borrower is only billed for the amount that is actually borrowed plus any interest due.

Options: An option is a contract which gives the buyer the right, but not the obligation, to buy or sell specified quantity of the underlying assets, at a specific (strike) price on or before a specified time (expiration date). The underlying may be a commodity like wheat or rice or financial instrument like equity stock or bonds etc. Options are basically of two types: call options and put options.

Call Options: A call option is an option to buy a stock at a specific price on or before a certain date. In this way, call options are like security deposits. If, for example, Mr. Wilson wants to rent a certain property, and leaves a security deposit for it, the money would be used to insure that he would, in fact, rent that property at the price agreed upon when he returns. If Mr. Wilson never returns, he would lose his security deposit, but he would have no other liability.

Call options usually increase in value as the value of the underlying instrument rises. When you buy a call option, the price you pay for it, called the option premium, secures your right to buy that certain stock at a specified price called the strike price. If you decide not to use the option to buy the stock, and you are not obligated to, your only cost is the *option premium.*

Put Options: Put options are options to sell a stock at a specific price on or before a certain date. In this way, put options are like insurance policies. If you buy a new car, and then buy auto insurance on the car, you pay a premium and are, hence, protected if the asset is damaged in an accident. If this happens, you can use your policy to regain the insured value of the car. In this way, the put option gains in value as the value of the underlying instrument decreases. If all goes well and the insurance is not needed, the insurance company keeps your premium in return for taking on the risk.

With a put option, you can *insure* a stock by fixing a selling price. If something happens which causes the stock price to fall, and thus, *damages* your asset, you can exercise your option and sell it at its *insured* price level. If the price of your stock goes up, and there is no *damage*, then you do not need to use the insurance, and, once again, your only cost is the premium.

Buying put options is buying insurance. To buy a put option on Nifty is to buy insurance which reimburses the full extent to which Nifty drops below the strike price of the put option. This is attractive to many people, and to mutual funds creating *guaranteed return products*. The Nifty index fund industry will find it very useful to make a bundle of a Nifty index fund and a Nifty put option to create a new kind of a Nifty index fund, which gives the investor protection against extreme drops in Nifty. Selling put options is selling insurance, so anyone who feels like earning revenues by selling insurance can set himself up to do so on the index options market.

Like forwards and futures, options represent another derivative instrument and provide a mechanism by which one can acquire a certain commodity or other asset in order to make profit or cover risk for a price. The options are similar to the future contracts in the sense that they are also standardized but are different from them in many ways. Options, in fact, represent the rights.

An option is the right, but not the obligation, to buy or sell a specified amount (and quality) of a commodity, currency, index, or financial instrument, or to buy or sell a specified number of underlying future contracts, at a specific price on or before a given date in future. Like other contracts, there are two parties to an option contract: the buyer who takes a long position and the seller or writer, who takes a short position. The option contract gives the owner a right to buy/sell a particular commodity or other asset at a specific pre-destined price by a specified date. The price involved is called exercise or strike price and the date involved is known as expiration. It is important to understand that such a contract gives its holder the right, and not the obligation to buy/sell. The option writer, on the other hand, undertakes upon himself the obligation to sell/buy the underlying asset if that suits the option holder. There is a wide variety of underlying assets including agricultural commodities, metals, shares, indices and so on, on which options are written.

Further, like future contracts, options are also tradable on exchanges. The exchange-traded options are standardized contracts and their trading is regulated by the exchanges that ensure the honouring of such contracts. Thus, in case of options as well, a clearing corporation takes the other side in every contract so that the party with the long position has a claim against the clearing corporation and the one with short position is obliged to it. However, buying or selling of future contracts does not require any price to be paid, called premium. The writer of an option receives the premium as a compensation of the risk that he takes upon himself. The premium belongs to the writer and is not adjusted in the price if the holder of the option decides to exercise it. This price is determined on the exchange, like the price of a share, by the forces of demand and supply. Further, like the share prices, the option prices also keep on changing with passage of time as trading takes place.

One difference between future and option trading may be noted. Whereas both parties to a future contract are required to deposit margins to the exchange, only the party with the short position is called upon to pay margin in case of options trading. The party with the long position does not pay anything beyond the premium.

Advantages of Option Trading: These are as under:

Risk Management: Put options allow investors holding shares to hedge against a possible fall in their value. This can be considered similar to taking out insurance against a fall in the share price.

Time to Decide: By taking a call option the purchase price for the shares is locked-in. This gives the call option holder until the expiry day to decide whether or not to exercise the option and buy the shares. Likewise, the taker of a put option has time to decide whether or not to sell the shares.

Speculation: The ease of trading in and out of an option position makes it possible to trade options with no intention of ever exercising them. If an investor expects the market to rise, he may decide to buy call options. If expecting a fall, he may decide to buy put options. Either way the holder can sell the option prior to expiry to take a profit or limit a loss. Trading options has a lower cost than shares, as there is no stamp duty payable unless and until options are exercised.

Leverage: Leverage provides the potential to make a higher return from a smaller initial outlay than investing directly. However, leverage usually involves more risks than a direct investment in the underlying shares. Trading in options can allow investors to benefit from a change in the price of the share without having to pay the full price of the share.

Income Generation: Shareholders can earn extra income over and above dividends by writing call options against their shares. By writing an option they receive the option premium upfront. While they get to keep the option premium, there is a possibility that they could be exercised against and have to deliver their shares to the taker at the exercise price.

Strategies: By combining different options, investors can create a wide range of potential profit scenarios.

Distinction between Futures and Options: Options are different from futures in several respects. At a practical level, the option buyer pays for the option in full at the time it is purchased. After this, he only has an upside. There is no possibility of the options position generating any further loss to him—other than the funds already paid for the option. Contrarily, futures are free to enter into but can generate very large losses. This feature makes options attractive to many occasional market participants who do not have time to monitor their futures positions.

More generally, options offer *non-linear payoffs* whereas futures only have *linear payoffs*. By combining futures and options, a wide variety of innovative and useful payoff structures can be created.

Pricing Options: Black-Scholes Formulae: An option buyer has the right but not the obligation to exercise on the seller. The worst that can happen to a buyer is the loss of the premium paid by him. His downside is limited to this premium, but his upside is potentially unlimited. This optionality is precious and has a value, which is expressed in terms of the option price. Just like in other free markets, it is the supply and demand in the secondary market that drives the price of an option.

There are various models which help us get close to the true price of an option. Most of these are variants of the celebrated Black-Scholes model for pricing European options. Today most calculators and spread-sheets come with a built-in Black-Scholes options pricing formula so to price options we do not really need to memorise the formula.

Options have existed—at least in concept—since antiquity. It was not until publication of the Black-Scholes (1973) option pricing formula that a theoretically consistent framework for pricing options became available. That framework was a direct result of work by Robert Merton as well as Fisher Black and Myron Scholes. In 1997, Scholes and Merton won the Nobel Prize in economics for this work. Black had died in 1995, but otherwise would have shared the prize.

The factors affecting the option price are the following:

1. Spot price of the underlying.
2. Exercise price.
3. Risk-free interest rate.
4. Volatility of the underlying.
5. Time to expiration.
6. Dividends on the underlying (stock or index).

Interestingly, before Black and Scholes came up with their option pricing model, there was a widespread belief that the expected growth of the underlying ought to affect the option price. Black and Scholes demonstrate that this is not true. The significance of the Black and Scholes model is that like any good model, it tells us what is important and what is not. It does not promise to produce the exact prices that show up in the market, but certainly does a remarkable job of pricing options within the framework of assumptions of the model. Virtually all option pricing models, even the most complex ones, have much in common with the Black-Scholes model.

Black and Scholes start by specifying a simple and well-known equation that models the way in which stock prices fluctuate. This equation called Geometric Brownian Motion, implies that stock returns will have a lognormal distribution, meaning that the logarithm of the stock's return will follow the normal (bell-shaped) distribution. Black and Scholes then propose that the option's price is determined by only two variables that are allowed to change: time and the underlying stock price. The other factors, namely the volatility, the exercise price, and the risk-free interest rate do affect the option's price but they are not allowed to change. By forming a portfolio consisting of a long position in stock and a short position in calls, the risk of the stock is eliminated. This hedged portfolio is obtained by setting the number of shares of stock equal to the approximate change in the call price for a changc in the stock price. This mix of stock and calls must be revised continuously, a process known as delta hedging.

Black and Scholes then turn to a little-known result in a specialised field of probability known as stochastic calculus. This result defines how the option price changes in terms of the change in the stock price and time to expiration. They then reason that this hedged combination of options and stock should grow in value at the risk-free rate. The result then is a partial differential equation. The solution is found by forcing a condition called a boundary condition on the model that requires the option price to converge to the exercise value at expiration. The end result is the Black and Scholes model.

Organization for Economic Co-operation and Development (OECD): It is an international organisation of industrialised nations with the following twofold objectives:

1. To contribute through co-operative efforts to economic growth, employment, financial stability and rising standard of

living in member countries.

2. To promote economic development of all nations and trade among them by assisting countries in their efforts to achieve these goals.

Based in Paris, OECD was formed on December 14, 1960 as a successor organisation to the Organisation for European Economic Co-operation (OEEC), whose main purpose was to co-ordinate the post-World War II economic recovery of Europe and to administer aid provided by US through the Marshall Plan. In addition to the 18 European members of the OEEC, US and Canada were among the original member countries. Since then, Australia, Finland, Japan and New Zealand have joined the organisation.

There are numerous committees and semiautonomous agencies that carry on the work of OECD. An indication of the multitude of topics covered by the OECD is given by the various committees which cover economic policy, energy, development assistance, technical co-operation, trade, international investment, multinational enterprises, insurance, financial markets, consumer affairs, tourism, sea transport, work force, education, environment, science, industry, agriculture and other areas of concern. Many of these committees have further subcommittees or working parties.

The following semi-autonomous agencies operate within the OECD framework: International Energy Agency created in 1974 to assist in the implementation of energy policies; Nuclear Energy Agency which was established in 1958 to promote the use of nuclear power for peaceful purposes; Development Centre, which has responsibilities in areas of research, liaison, information exchange and expert assistance related to development problems; Road Research Programme; Educational Research and Innovation Centre; and Interfutures Project, which is a long-range study and analysis group.

Among the wide variety of functions and tasks performed by the OECD are the collection and dissemination of statistical information on the member countries and conduct of basic research and policy studies. The Secretariat maintains extensive data bank and publishes relevant statistical information on the member countries. It also engages in regular economic forecasting exercises and publishes their findings. On a more formal level, the OECD Council may adopt decisions which are binding upon member countries or recommendations for their voluntary consideration and possible implementation.

Organization of Petroleum Exporting Countries (OPEC): It is an association of the world's oil-producing countries. Formed in 1960, its headquarters are in Vienna, Austria. The chief purpose of OPEC is to coordinate the petroleum policies of its members: Algeria, Ecuador, Gabon, Indonesia, Iran, Iraq, Kuwait, Libya, Nigeria, Qatar, Saudi Arabia, the United Arab Emirates, and Venezuela.

Outsourcing by Banks

The term outsourcing may be defined as use of a third party (either an affiliated entity within a corporate group or an entity that is external to the corporate group) to perform activities on a continuing basis that would normally be undertaken by the bank itself. Third party or service provider refers to the entity that is undertaking the outsourced activity on behalf of the bank. There are some key risks in outsourcing such as strategic risk, reputation risk, compliance risk, operational risk, exit strategy risk, counterparty risk, country risk, contractual risk, access risk, concentration risk and systemic risk. It would be imperative for the bank outsourcing its activities to ensure effective management of these risks.

The failure of a service provider in providing a specified service, a breach in security/ confidentiality, or non-compliance with legal and regulatory requirements by either the service provider or the outsourcing bank can lead to financial losses for the bank and could also lead to systemic risks within the entire banking system in the country. Hence, its board of directors and management of bank need to provide direction and guidance to banks to adopt sound and responsive risk management practices for effective oversight, due diligence and management of risks arising out of such outsourcing activities.

Some outsourcing arrangements, if disrupted, have the potential to significantly impact bank's business operations, reputation or profitability. Such arrangements are considered 'material outsourcing'. Banks should use qualitative judgement to assess whether or not an outsourcing arrangement that is in existence or being planned, is to be considered 'material outsourcing' or not.

Before entering into, or significantly changing, an outsourcing arrangement, a bank should: (i) analyse how the arrangement will fit into its organisation and reporting structure; (ii) consider whether the agreement establishing the outsourcing arrangement will allow it to monitor and control its operational risk exposure relating to the service provider; (iii) conduct appropriate due diligence of the service provider's financial position and expertise; (iv) consider how it will ensure a smooth transition of its operations from its current arrangements to a new or changed outsourcing arrangement (including what will happen on the termination of the contract); and (v) consider any concentration risk implications such as the business continuity implications that may arise if a single service provider is used by several banks.

The bank should require its service providers to develop and establish a robust framework for documenting, maintaining and testing business continuity and recovery procedures. Outsourcing often leads to the sharing of facilities operated by the service provider. The bank should ensure that service providers are able to isolate the bank's information, documents and records, and other assets. This is to ensure that in adverse conditions, all documents, records of transactions and information given to the service provider, and assets of the bank can be removed from the possession of the service provider in order to continue its business operations, or deleted, destroyed or rendered unusable.

The bank should have in place a management structure to monitor and control its outsourcing activities. A bank that has entered into or is planning material outsourcing, or is planning to vary any such outsourcing arrangements, should adhere to the regulatory and supervisory requirements. It is imperative for the bank, when performing its due diligence in relation to outsourcing, to consider all relevant laws, regulations, guidelines and conditions of approval, licensing or registration. The engagement of service providers in a foreign country exposes a bank to country risk - economic, social and political conditions and events in a foreign country that may adversely affect the bank. Such conditions and events could prevent the service provider from carrying out the terms of its agreement with the bank. To manage the country risk involved in such outsourcing activities, the bank should take into account and closely monitor government policies and political, social, economic and legal conditions in countries where the service provider is based.

Outstanding Cheque: A cheque written by a depositor that has not yet been presented for payment to or paid by the depositor's bank.

Overdraft: When the amount of money withdrawn from a bank account is greater than the amount actually available in the account, the excess is known as an overdraft, and the account is said to be overdrawn.

Overdraw: To write a cheque for an amount that exceeds the amount on deposit in the account.

Over-the-counter: It is a figurative term for the means of trading securities which are not listed on an organised stock exchange. Over-the-counter trading is done by broker-dealers who communicate by telephone and computer networks.

Pp

Par Value: The official fixed exchange rate between two currencies or between a currency and a specific weight of gold or a basket of currencies.

Passbook: A book in ledger form in which are recorded all deposits, withdrawals, and earnings of a customer's savings account.

Past Due Item: Any note or other time instrument of indebtedness that has not been paid on the due date.

Pay-As-You-Earn (PAYE): It is a system of collecting income tax at source from employees recommended by British economist J.M. Keynes and introduced in Britain in 1944. See also Withholding Tax.

Payee: The person or organization to whom a cheque, draft, or note is made payable.

Payer: The person or organization who pays.

Paying Bank: A bank upon which a cheque is drawn and that pays a cheque or other draft.

Payment and Settlement Systems: The payment and settlement systems are at the core of financial infrastructure in a country. A well-functioning payment and settlement system is crucial for the successful implementation of monetary policy and maintaining the financial stability. Central banks have, therefore, always maintained a keen interest in the development of payment and settlement system as part of their responsibilities for monetary and financial stability. In India, the development of a safe, secure and sound payment and settlement system has been the key policy objective. In this direction, the RBI, apart from performing the regulatory and supervisory functions, has also been making efforts to promote functionality and modernisation of the payment and settlement systems on an on-going basis.

A safe and efficient payment system is a prerequisite for smooth functioning of the financial markets. The conduct of monetary policy in an effective manner requires safe and efficient payment and settlement systems to facilitate transfer of funds and securities between the central bank and other participants in the financial system. An efficient and stable payment and settlement system is also a pre-condition for inter-bank money markets and other short-term credit markets through which monetary policy is transmitted. In addition, developments in the payment and settlement systems that affect the speed and realisation/availability of funds for further deployment can influence the overall demand for money in the economy.

By linking financial institutions together for the purpose of transferring monetary claims and settling payment obligations, payment and settlement system becomes a channel through which financial risks are transmitted across financial institutions and markets. Well-designed and efficiently managed systems, therefore, help in maintaining financial stability by reducing uncertainty of settlement. Settlement failures which spread to other payment and settlement systems through the contagion effect not only undermine the smooth functioning of the financial markets, but can also adversely affect the public confidence in money and efficacy of the instruments used to transfer money.

Central banks world-wide are involved in payment and settlement systems in a number of ways. They provide settlement accounts, oversee core payment arrangements, and operate, provide and use various payment services.

In India, RBI regulates and supervises payment and settlement systems with the objective of promoting safety and efficiency by monitoring the existing and planned systems, assessing them against the stated objectives and, where necessary, inducing change. The oversight of payment and settlement systems has become more distinct and formal in recent years as part of a growing concern with financial stability as also with the increasing role of private participants in financial transactions. The increasing attention by the RBI also reflects the large increase in the value of transfers cleared and settled, the increasing centralisation of transactions around a small number of key systems and the growing technological complexity.

Payment Due Date: The date on which a loan or instalment payment is due. It is set by a financial institution. Any payment received after this date is considered late, and fees and penalties can be assessed.

Payoff: The complete repayment of a loan, including principal, interest, and any other amounts due. Payoff occurs either over the full term of the loan or through pre-payments.

Payoff Statement: A formal statement prepared when a loan payoff is contemplated. It shows the current status of the loan account, all sums due, and the daily rate of interest.

Periodic Rate: The interest rate described in relation to a specific amount of time. The monthly periodic rate, for example, is the cost of credit per month, and the daily periodic rate is the cost of credit per day.

Periodic Statement: The billing summary produced and mailed at specified intervals, usually monthly.

Periodicity: It refers to the frequency with which the data are compiled. Periodicity specifications for flow data are given in terms of the longest interval to be represented by a single data point, and those for stock data are given in the form of the longest interval between compilations. For example, the specification of quarterly periodicity for balance of payments data means that one quarter is the longest interval that may be represented by a single estimate.

Perpetual Inventory Method: The process of deriving data on stocks from transaction data is known as the perpetual inventory method. Under this method, for which a stock estimate for some base point in time is required, the compiler may calculate the value of a stock at the end of a period as being equal to the value of the stock at the beginning of the period, plus the impact of transactions and non-transaction changes in the value of the stock during the period.

Perquisite: It means any casual emolument or benefit attached to an office or position in addition to salary or wages. Perquisites may be provided in cash or in kind.

Personal Identification Number (PIN): Generally, a four-character number or word, the PIN is the secret code given to credit or debit cardholders enabling them to access their accounts. The code is either randomly assigned by the bank or selected by the customer. It is intended to prevent unauthorized use of the card while accessing a financial service terminal.

Portfolio: It refers to the list of investments in shares, debentures, bonds etc. that a person or an institution has made.

Portfolio Investment: In general, any foreign investment that is not direct investment is considered portfolio investment. Foreign portfolio investment includes the purchase of securities (stocks), bonds, trade finance, and government lending or borrowing, excluding transactions in official reserves. See also Foreign Direct Investment.

Positioning: It is a recent term used by transnational corporations (TNCs) for perceiving new positions in new countries/ventures so as to judge their sustainable competitive advantage. Positioning can be of the following types:

Access-based Positioning: It refers to a systematic study by a TNC of a country's geography, resource base, market, policy environment etc.

Need-based Positioning: It is like serving most or all the needs of a particular group of customers.

Variety-based Positioning: It refers to a TNC producing a subset of a firm's products/services.

Power of Attorney: A written instrument which authorizes one person to act as another's agent or attorney. The power of attorney may be for a definite, specific act, or it may be general in nature. The terms of the written power of attorney may specify when it will expire. If not, the power of attorney usually expires when the person granting it dies.

Pre-authorized Payment: A system established by a written agreement under which a financial institution is authorized by the customer to debit the customer's account in order to pay bills or make loan payments.

Preference Shares: It is a class of shares with a claim on the company's earnings before payment is made on the common shares. Preference shares are normally entitled to dividend at a fixed rate which depends on the terms of the issue. Preference shares are usually entitled to priority if the company is liquidated.

Premium: A regular payment paid for an insurance policy that provides protection against a risk.

Pre-payment: The payment of a debt before it actually becomes due.

Pre-payment Clause: A clause in a mortgage allowing the mortgagor to pay off part or all of the unpaid debt before it becomes due.

Pre-payment Penalty: A penalty imposed on a borrower for repaying the loan before its due date (in the case of a mortgage, this applies when there is not a prepayment clause in the mortgage note to offset the penalty).

Previous Year and Assessment Year: Under the Indian Income Tax Act, 1961, the year during which the income is received or otherwise earned is called previous year (i.e. the income year). It is a period of 12 months starting from April 1 of every year and ending on March 31 of the next year. This is also the financial year of the Government of India. The year immediately succeeding the previous year and in which the income so earned is assessed to tax is called the assessment year (i.e. the tax year). For example, income for the period from April 1, 2013 to March 31, 2014 (i.e. 2013-14) is income of the previous year relevant for the assessment year 2014-15.

Price-earning Ratio: It is the ratio of the price of a share to its earnings. It is the most widely accepted guide to determine whether or not to buy or sell shares. Firms with good growth rates often earn high profits and hence record a high P/E ratio.

Primary and Secondary Securities: Primary securities are created by real sector units of the economy (joint stock companies) engaged in the production of goods. Shares and debentures issued by companies are good examples of primary securities. Secondary securities are created by financial institutions or intermediaries who are not the ultimate borrowers of funds. These institutions raise funds from public to make investments in primary securities. Some examples of secondary securities are bank deposits, units of Unit Trust of India and shares of mutual funds.

Principal Balance: The outstanding balance on a loan, excluding interest and fees.

Prior Deposits: A deposit required by a government of a specified sum, in domestic or foreign currency, usually corresponding to a certain percentage of the value of the imported product. Such deposits are characteristically held without interest, sometimes for many months—from the time an order is placed until after the import transaction is completed—and hence represent a real cost to the importer. The purpose of prior deposits is usually to discourage imports, particularly for balance-of-payments reasons, and they generally are recognized as non-tariff barriers that impede trade. Prior deposits must usually be made at the time an import license is granted.

Private Company and Public Limited Company: Private company means a company which: (a) restricts the right to transfer its shares, (b) limits the number of its members to fifty, and (c) prohibits any invitation to the public to subscribe for any shares in the company. The violation of these conditions will make it a public limited company.

Private Placement: The term refers to sale/issue of securities to an institutional investor through direct contact.

Privatisation: The term privatisation conveys a variety of ideas: (a) outright denationalisation, (b) diluting public sector capital holding, (c) allowing private sector in areas hitherto reserved for public sector, and (d) general deregulation and liberalisation of industrial and trade activities.

Public Corporation: A public corporation is created by a special law defining its objectives, powers, and privileges. Except for appropriations to provide capital or to cover losses, it is usually independently financed. It derives revenues from the sale of goods and services and can also borrow from the Government and from the public. Employees of a public corporation are not civil servants.

Public Debt: Public debt is a method by which governments obtain money. Public debts are incurred through public loans. A loan may be either voluntary or compulsory. A government may raise loans either internally or externally. Clearly, external loans are voluntary in nature. Public loans may be for short, medium or long period. Short-term loans are also known as *floating debt.* Long term loans are also called *funded debt.* Public borrowings involve problems of debt management which is clearly related to monetary policy. The payment of interest on and the repayment of principal of public debt (debt servicing) form part of public expenditure. Public debts, unlike taxes, leave behind liabilities for future generations.

Purchasing Power: The ability of consumers to acquire goods and services based on their possession of money and/or their recourse to credit. Aggregate purchasing power within a market or a national economy reflects total disposable income after taxes, and hence the level of employment.

Put Options: See Options, *169*.

Qq

Quasi Corporations: These are enterprises that produce goods and services in an economy other than their own, but do not establish separate legal corporations in the host country. Quasi-corporations that are in a direct investment relationship with the parent enterprise are deemed to exist if: (a) production is maintained for one year or more, (b) a separate set of accounts is maintained for the local activities, and (c) income tax is paid in the host country. Quasi-corporations are often involved in construction or the operation of mobile equipment in another economy.

Quota: It fixes a limit on the amount of a particular item that may be exported/imported during a given period of time. As an instrument of trade policy, quotas provide more effective protection for domestic producers than a comparably restrictive tariff. However, quotas do not generate additional tax revenue.

Quotation: A quotation represents the price and conditions at which a seller is prepared to supply goods.

Rr

RBI: See Reserve Bank of India, *191*.

Recession: It means a substantial drop in the level of economic activities in an economy.

Reconciliation: The process of analyzing two related records and, if differences exist between them, finding the cause and bringing the two records into agreement. For example, comparing an up-to-date cheque book with a monthly statement from the financial institution holding the account.

Redlining: The alleged practice of certain lending institutions of not making mortgage, home improvement, and small business loans in certain neighbourhoods—usually areas that are deteriorating or considered by the lender to be poor investments.

Re-export: It refers to export of previously imported goods without additional processing or alteration. If they remain at a free port or bonded warehouse, such goods usually are not subject to import duty.

Refinancing: A way of obtaining a better interest rate, lower monthly payments, or borrow cash on the equity in a property that has built up on a loan. A second loan is taken out to pay off the first, higher-rate loan.

Refund: An amount paid back because of an overpayment or because of the return of an item previously sold.

Regional Rural Banks (RRBs): RRBs form an important segment of the rural financial sector. They were conceived as institutions that combine the local feel and familiarity of the co-operatives with the business capabilities of commercial banks.

This sector has an exclusive role in improving financial inclusion and catering to vital sectors like agriculture and allied economic activities. Public policy, therefore, aims at keeping this sector viable and strong through various forms of active intervention.

Nature and Objectives of RRBs: Agriculture and rural sectors play an important role in India's overall development strategy in terms of income and employment generation and poverty alleviation. Great significance has, therefore, been accorded to developing appropriate institutions and mechanisms for catering to the credit requirements of these sectors.

Despite the measures taken by the Government of India and the RBI—including nationalisation of 14 major commercial banks in 1969—a large proportion of the rural poor continued to be outside the banking fold. A Working Group (Chairman: M. Narasimham) was set up in 1975 to explore the possibilities of evolving an alternative rural credit agency to benefit the rural poor. The Group recommended formation of a new set of regionally-oriented rural banks which would combine the local feel and familiarity of rural problems characteristic of cooperatives and the professionalism and large resource base of commercial banks. RRBs were set up as a sequel to this recommendation.

RRBs have a special place in the multi-agency approach adopted to provide agricultural and rural credit in India. These banks were established under the Regional Rural Banks Act, 1976 "with a view to developing the rural economy by providing, for the purpose of development of agriculture, trade, commerce, industry and other productive activities in the rural areas, credit and other facilities, particularly to small and marginal farmers, agricultural labourers, artisans and small entrepreneurs, and for matters connected therewith and incidental thereto".

The capital of RRBs is contributed by the Union Government, concerned State Government and a sponsor bank in the ratio 50:15:35. RRBs have played a key role in rural institutional financing in terms of geographical coverage, clientele outreach, business volume and contribution to the development of the rural economy. As on March 31, 2013, there were 64 RRBs with a total of 17,856 branches covering 635 districts in the country.

Besides the RRBs, commercial and co-operative banks have been catering to the credit requirements of the rural sector. While the commercial banks, with their focus on profitability had certain limitations in accelerating agricultural credit, the cooperative banks efforts were also hampered by several financial weaknesses.

Though over the years the RRBs have been able to expand their outreach and business and meet the credit requirements of the poor, several weaknesses have emerged, eroding their profitability and viability. The recent focus of the Government of India on doubling the flow of credit to the agricultural sector has warranted a re-look at the relative roles of co-operative banks, RRBs and commercial banks.

As the very objective of setting up RRBs was to extend adequate credit to the rural borrowers and particularly the economically weaker sections, owing to their rural orientation, there is a growing realization that RRBs could be used as an effective vehicle for credit delivery in the rural areas. There is, therefore, a need to devise ways and means to improve the health and viability of RRBs so as to reposition them in the credit delivery mechanism in India.

Reinsurance: The shifting by agreement (known in the insurance industry as a *treaty*) of part of the risk (or *exposure*) of the original insurer (the ceding company) to another insurer (the reinsurer). Sometimes a reinsurer will, in turn, pass on part of its risk to another reinsurer through a process known as retrocession.

Release of Lien: To free a piece of real estate from a mortgage.

Renewal: A form of extending an unpaid loan in which the borrower's remaining unpaid loan balance is carried over (renewed) into a new loan at the beginning of the next financing period.

Repo: See Repurchase Option (Repo), *191*.

Repurchase Option (Repo): Reserve Bank of India (RBI) is able to influence short-term interest rates by modulating the liquidity in the system through repo operations under the liquidity adjustment facility (LAF), reinforced by interest rate signals. RBI enforces the interest rate corridor defined by the reverse repo rate, i.e. the price at which it absorbs liquidity and the repo rate/Bank rate, i.e. the price at which it injects liquidity into the system. In other words, repo rate is the rate at which RBI repurchases government securities from banks. In return, banks get cash to meet their short-term requirements. When RBI wants to inject liquidity in the system it reduces the repo rate which also acts as the benchmark short-term lending rate. Reverse repo is a mirror image of repo.

Reputational Risk: Banks have long based their business on a reputation of trust. A bank's reputation can be adversely impacted if it fails to respond to inquiries, does not provide proper disclosure, or violates customer privacy. A bank's reputation can be damaged by Internet banking services that are poorly executed or otherwise alienate customers and the public.

Reserve Bank of India (RBI): The Reserve Bank of India Act was placed on the statute book on March 6, 1934. The RBI commenced operations on April 1, 1935 and was nationalised on January 1, 1949. The head office of the Bank is in Mumbai and its executive head is called the Governor.

The objective of establishing the RBI, as stated in the preamble to the RBI Act 1934, was to "regulate the issue of bank notes and the keeping of the reserves with a view to securing monetary stability in India and generally to operate the currency and credit system of the country to its advantage". The Bank's functions as laid down in the statutes were: (a) issue of currency, (b) banker to Government, and (c) banker to other banks. Except in the sphere of agriculture, the Bank was not entrusted with any great promotional role and that too on a limited scale.

Functions of RBI: The RBI performs all the major functions of a central bank and these are discussed below.

***Sole Currency Authority*:** Barring one-rupee notes and coins, RBI is the sole authority for the issue of currency in India. One rupee notes and coins are issued by the Central Government. However, their distribution to the public is the sole responsibility of the RBI. For the issue of notes, the RBI has a separate department, the Department of Issue. All the currency issued by the RBI is its monetary liability and is backed by assets of equal value.

Banker to the Governments: Before the formation of the RBI, the Imperial Bank of India performed many of the functions as banker to the Government. With the establishment of the RBI, the Imperial Bank ceased to be the banker to the Government, but entered into an agreement with the RBI for providing its services as the sole agent of the RBI in places where it had a branch and there was no branch of the Banking Dcpartment of the RBI.

As the banker to the Central Government and to the State Governments by virtue of agreements entered into with them, the RBI provides a range of banking services for these Governments such as acceptance of money on government account payment/withdrawals of funds and collection and transfer of funds through different means. Sections 20, 21 and 21A of the RBI Act provide the statutory basis for these functions. The terms and conditions on which the RBI acts as banker to the Central and State Governments are set out in separate agreements, which the RBI entered into with these Governments.

Presently, RBI is the banker for all Governments in India (except Jammu and Kashmir). The RBI provides all those banking services to the Central and State Governments which a commercial bank ordinarily offers to its customers. The Governments keep their cash balances on current account deposit with the RBI and the latter carries out banking business involving receipts and payments of money on behalf of the Governments. The Governments are required, under agreement, to maintain a minimum balance with the RBI. It is the duty of the Finance Department of each Government to ensure that there are always sufficient funds in its bank account and that at no stage the cash balance falls short of the prescribed minimum.

Bankers' Bank and Lender-of-the-last-resort: Under the Reserve Bank of India Act, 1934 and the Banking Regulation Act, 1949, the RBI is vested with extensive powers of supervision, regulation, and control over commercial and co-operative banks. The regulatory functions of the RBI pertain to licensing, branch expansion, and amalgamation of commercial banks. The RBI calls for returns and other information from the commercial banks and periodically inspects their working.

The scheduled banks in India are required under law to deposit with the RBI a stipulated ratio (lying between 3 percent and 15 percent) of their total liabilities. These are compulsory reserves of banks with the RBI and are not available to them for meeting inter-bank clearing claims. The underlying philosophy of this statutory reserve requirement is that by varying it within limits, the RBI can use it as a weapon of monetary-credit control.

Reserves of the banks with the RBI may be used to meet the temporary cash needs of the commercial banks. Commercial banks are supposed to meet their shortfalls of cash from sources other than the RBI but in acute emergency they can approach the RBI for help and that is why the central bank is also called the lender-of-the-last-resort.

Controller of Money and Credit: An important function of RBI is to control money and credit in the country. The instruments of monetary control operated by the RBI may be classified into two categories: (a) quantitative or global or aggregative measures which affect the total amount of money supply and credit, and (b) qualitative or selective measures which affect the allocation of bank credit among competing uses and users.

A. Quantitative Credit Controls: These are the following.

1. **Bank Rate:** As the lender-of-the-last-resort, the RBI helps the commercial banks in temporary need of cash when other

sources of raising cash are exhausted. The RBI provides credit to banks by rediscounting eligible bills of exchange and by making advances against eligible securities such as government securities. The lending rate for these advances by the RBI is called the bank rate which is a traditional weapon to control money supply. An increase in the bank rate would discourage commercial banks to borrow from the RBI and a corresponding increase in the lending rate of commercial banks to general public would decrease public borrowings from the banks.

2. **Cash Reserve Ratio (CRR)**: Scheduled banks in India are required statutorily to hold cash reserves, called cash reserve ratio (CRR), with the RBI. Increase/decrease in CRR is used by the RBI as an instrument of monetary control, particularly to mop up excess increases in the supply of money. This power was given to RBI in 1956.
3. **Statutory Liquidity Ratio (SLR):** Apart from the CRR, banks in India are also subject to statutory liquidity requirement. Under this requirement, commercial banks along with other financial institutions like Life Insurance Corporation of India, the General Insurance Corporation and the provident funds are required under law to invest prescribed minimum proportions of their total assets/liabilities in government securities and other approved securities. The underlying philosophy of this provision is to allocate total bank credit between the government and the rest of the economy. The assurance of a certain minimum share of bank credit to the government affects the borrowings of the government from the RBI and hence serves as a tool of quantitative monetary control. The SLR provision has created a captive market for government securities which increases automatically with the growth in the liabilities of the banks. Moreover, it has kept the cost of the debt to the government low in view of the generally low rate of interest on government securities.
4. **Open Market Operations:** The RBI can enter the money

market for the purpose of purchase or sale of Government securities on its own account. Every open market purchase by the RBI increases primary money by equal amount while every sale decreases it. As regards their advantages, open market operations are highly flexible, easily reversible in time, their effect on money supply is immediate, and they do not carry *announcement effects* as in the case of changes in the bank rate. Open market operations, considered very effective in developed countries, are not of much importance in India in view of the captive nature of the market for Government bonds. For example, the treasury bill market is limited largely to the RBI itself and scheduled commercial banks which are required under law to invest a certain minimum proportion of their total liabilities in Government securities. The private dealers in Government securities are few and far between.

5. **Moral Suasions:** Through moral suasions (discussions, suggestions and advice), the RBI can influence the investment and credit policies of the commercial banks. For example, it can ask the commercial banks to invest a larger proportion, than required, of their assets in Government securities. Similarly, it can advise them regarding the allocation of credit to the private sector.

B. Selective Credit Controls (SCCs): SCCs, introduced in India in 1956, pertain to regulation of credit for specific purposes. The techniques of SCCs used by the RBI include fixing minimum margins for lending against securities, ceiling on maximum advances to individual borrowers against stocks of certain commodities, and minimum discriminatory rates of interest prescribed for certain kinds of advances. SCCs have been used mainly to prevent the speculative holding of essential commodities like foodgrains to prevent price rise.

Selective credit controls were abolished in the wake of economic reforms programme initiated in early 1990s.

Controller of Foreign Exchange: The RBI is the custodian of the foreign exchange reserves of India. It manages exchange control and the external value of the rupee. The history of exchange control in India dates back to the outbreak of Second World War in 1939. The exchange control is operated in a manner so that the demand for foreign exchange is contained within the limits of its available supplies. In other words, the available foreign exchange is allocated among competing demands in such a way as to make its optimum use. The need for this control and planned use arises in view of the general shortage of foreign exchange reserves in most developing countries. All foreign exchange transactions made by the RBI are at the official rates of exchange.

The RBI has delegated considerable powers to the authorised dealers to release foreign exchange for a variety of purposes and has been focusing on the development of the foreign exchange market. In order to deepen the foreign exchange market, a large number of products have been introduced and the entry of newer players has been allowed. Additional hedging instruments, such as, foreign currency-rupee options have been introduced and authorised dealers have been permitted to use innovative products like cross-currency options, interest rate and currency swaps, caps/collars and forward rate agreements (FRAs) in the international forex market.

Source of Economic Information: The RBI provides, through its publications, useful data and information on various aspects of the economy, particularly monetary and banking activities. Three important and regular publications of the RBI are: (a) Reserve Bank of India *Bulletin* (Monthly), (b) *Report on Currency and Finance* (Annual), and (c) *Handbook of Statistics on Indian Economy.*

Promotional Role of RBI: Apart from performing the customary functions of a central bank, the RBI has played an important role in building, consolidating, and strengthening the financial infrastructure of India. It has also played an effective role in influencing the allocation of credit in favour of priority sectors. Commercial banking facilities have been extended to small towns and rural areas as a result of the policies of the RBI.

The RBI has paid special attention to the credit needs of the rural (agricultural) sector. Towards this end, the Agricultural Refinance and Development Corporation (ARDC) was set up as a wholly-owned subsidiary of the RBI in 1963. The National Bank for Agriculture and Rural Development (NABARD) is another example of the promotional role of the RBI in the agricultural sector. Similarly, the RBI promoted the cause of industrial finance by actively associating itself with such public sector undertakings as erstwhile Industrial Development Bank of India (IDBI). In the area of credit allocation, RBI has followed the policy of special consideration for priority sectors at concessional rates of interest. See also Central Bank.

Reserve Currency: It refers to currency such as the dollar or pound sterling, or international currency such as special drawing rights (SDRs), used by many countries to settle debit balances in their international accounts. Central banks generally hold a large portion of their monetary reserves in reserve currencies, which are sometimes called *key* currencies.

Reserves: It is the money from profits not paid as dividend and which is retained by a company to be used later for purposes which the directors think fit.

Residential Status: In the tax laws of most countries, income which is subject to charge of tax varies according to the residential status of a taxpayer. Generally, a resident taxpayer is charged to income tax on his world income, subject to a double taxation relief in respect of foreign incomes taxed abroad. However, a non-resident is charged income tax only on incomes received, accruing, or arising in that country. Tax laws generally lay down rules defining when a person is to be treated as resident or non-resident.

Resurgent India Bonds (RIBs), 1998: The issue of RIBs was contemplated in view of extraordinary developments in 1998-99, when a shortfall in capital flows consequent upon imposition of sanctions, especially debt flows, in relation to current account deficit was anticipated. Instead of drawing down foreign exchange reserves which could have adversely affected market sentiments, or reducing the current account deficit through drastic import cuts which would have affected real economic activity, it was felt that RIBs would enhance the debt flows at the least possible cost. It was envisaged that such borrowings could offset the adverse market sentiment created in international capital markets in the light of the downgrading of India's sovereign rating to non-investment grade. This could have been done by demonstrably raising debt resources at a cost lower than that any organised financial intermediary was prepared to provide in the context of the rating downgrade. At the same time, it was necessary to ensure that amounts so obtained were restricted quantitatively to meet essential needs as a replacement for normal debt flows, by keeping an option for premature closure.

Furthermore, by keeping the maturity of RIBs to five years, it was ensured that the borrowing had an appropriate medium-term maturity. The success of RIBs could be gauged from the substantial amount of funds mobilised (US$ 4.2 billion) in the international market at, a competitive rate. The RIBs were redeemed on October 1, 2003 without any pressure on the exchange rate and liquidity conditions.

Return Item: A negotiable instrument—principally a cheque—that has been sent to one bank for collection and payment and is returned unpaid by the sending bank.

Revenue Expenditure: It relates to the normal running of an organisation. Broadly speaking, all those expenditures of an organisation which do not result in the creation of physical or financial assets are treated as revenue expenditures. See also Capital Expenditure.

Revenue Receipts: Moneys obtained in the normal course of business are called revenue receipts, e.g. sale proceeds, interest on deposits, and dividends on investment. Revenue receipts are normally of recurring nature and are not meant for any specific purpose. See also Capital Receipts.

Reverse Repo: See Repurchase Option (Repo), *191*.

Revocable Letter of Credit: See Letter of Credit, *141*.

Risk Based Supervision (RBS): Considering the complexities of banking business and emerging product innovations with complex risk profiles, the RBI initiated measures to implement RBS approach to the supervision.

The RBS approach is based on the principle of differentiated supervision. Banks are differentiated on the basis of their risk profiles and the risks posed by them to the stability of the financial system. Banks with high risk, and within the banks, critical areas with high risk, receive more supervisory attention. The RBS thus helps in allocating supervisory resources more efficiently and focusing supervisory attention according to the risk profile of each institution. Evaluation of risk management systems in banks is the essence of the RBS.

Several initiatives have been taken by the RBI for a gradual roll out of the RBS process. There were two rounds of pilot run of RBS covering 23 banks in public sector, private sector (old and new) and foreign banks categories during 2003-2005. Evaluation of the findings of first pilot run revealed that the bank level preparedness for RBS/risk based internal audit (RBIA) process was very slow. There were certain overlaps under both the business and control risks. Several steps were, therefore, taken to streamline the RBS process.

First, pending amendment to risk profile templates, changes were made in the structure of inspection report to capture and report business risk and control risk in one place. Second, a work book together with a sample on-site inspection report was designed to help the inspecting officers to undertake the RBS.

Third, a resource group with officers from different departments of the RBI is in existence to analyse various risk models employed by banks in India.

Risk Management: Risk management in any type of institution is a continuous process and not a one-time activity. It has three distinctive sequential steps: (a) risk identification, (b) risk measurement, and (c) risk mitigation.

Risk can be defined as the possibility and probability of loss. These are: (a) credit risk, (b) market risk, and (c) operational risk.

Derivatives can be used to hedge both credit and market risks. While credit risk represents the conventional counter party risk, market risk refers to all those market forces/variables which may adversely affect an institution's profitability and economic value. Market risk is characteristically represented by price risk of all types, viz. interest rate risk, exchange rate risk, commodity price risk, equity price risk etc. While credit and market risks are external, operational risks are those risks which are essentially internal to an organization. Derivatives are of little help in hedging such types of risks.

Runaway Capital: It refers to that investment which is made abroad instead of at home. It, therefore, involves loss to the domestic economy in terms of employment and income generation. Multinational corporations are often accused of encouraging this type of investment.

Rural Co-operatives: Historically, rural co-operative credit institutions have played an important role in providing institutional credit to the agricultural and rural sectors. The structure of rural co-operative banks is not uniform across all the States of the country. Some States have a unitary structure with the State level banks operating through their own branches, while others have a mixed structure incorporating both unitary and federal systems.

These credit institutions, based on the nature of their lending operations, have typically been divided into two distinct segments, viz. short-term cooperative credit institutions and long-term co-operative credit institutions.

Short-term Rural Co-operatives: The short-term provide crop and other working capital loans to farmers and rural artisans primarily for short-term purposes. These credit institutions have a federal three-tier structure: (i) at the apex of the system is a state co-operative bank (SCB) in each State; (ii) at the middle (or district) level, there are district central co-operative banks (DCCBs) also known as district co-operative banks; and (iii) at the lowest (or village) level are the primary agricultural credit societies (PACS). The smaller States and Union Territories (UTs) have a two-tier structure with SCBs directly meeting the credit requirements of PACS.

Long-term Rural Co-operatives: They provide medium and long-term loans for making investments in agriculture, rural industries and, in the recent period, housing.

Ss

Safe Deposit Box: A type of safe usually located in groups inside a bank vault and rented to customers for their use in storing valuable items.

Safekeeping: A service provided by banks where securities and valuables are protected in the vaults of the bank for customers.

Sales Tax: It is normally an *ad valorem* levy imposed on the seller with reference to the transaction of sale. Sales tax is generally regressive in nature because being paid by all consumers, it takes a larger proportion of small incomes than of larger ones. On the basis of the stage of collection, sales tax is classified into: (a) multi-point sales tax, and (b) single-point sales tax.

Satellite Banking: Having regard to much greater reliability of a satellite-based communication link for interconnecting the branches of the banks, particularly in the hilly areas and difficult terrain where terrestrial communication link is difficult to provide, the RBI had constituted a technical group to examine the proposal for providing satellite connectivity to the bank branches in such areas. The objective is to enable greater penetration of the electronic payment products in the hinterland areas also, by facilitating the integration of the rural and remote branches with the core banking solution platform of the banks and help them providing efficient banking services to their customers.

Under the proposal, the RBI would be bearing a part of the leased rentals for the satellite connectivity, provided the banks use it for connecting their branches in the North Eastern States and in the under-banked districts in the rest of the country. Thus, the RBI would be providing an incentive to the banks for adopting the satellite communication technology for networking their branches in the remote areas.

Scheduled and Non-scheduled Banks: See Commercial Bank, *37*.

Scrutiny Assessment: It arises where an assessing officer considers it necessary to ensure that the assessee has not: (a) understated his income, (b) returned excessive loss, or (c) underpaid the tax. He may serve a notice on the assessee requiring him to appear on the specified date or to furnish any document/evidence in support of his return.

There are various factors guiding the selection of a case for scrutiny. Some of these are: (a) continuous losses from year to year, (b) low profitability declared compared to the general profitability in similar business, (c) extraordinary expenditure booked, and (d) huge private borrowings made.

Search and Seizure: The term refers to the powers of tax authorities to obtain tax-related information in the possession of a taxpayer which is not otherwise being disclosed. Tax officials are vested with considerable powers to carry out search operations. To conduct a search (popularly called raid) and seizure, an authorisation in the prescribed form is issued by the competent tax authority under his signature and seal. Under Sections 132 and 132A of the Indian Income Tax Act, 1961, a search party can: (a) enter and search any building, place or vehicle in occupation of the person being searched, (b) break the lock and examine any box, locker, cupboard etc., and (c) seize any books of account, other documents, money, bullion, jewellery etc.

Securities: Generically, the term includes shares, bonds, debentures etc. of any body corporate or government. Securities which appear on the official stock exchange list and which may be bought and sold on the stock exchange are called listed securities. Definitive securities are paper certificates and book-entry securities are electronic records evidencing ownership of equity, bonds etc.

Securities and Exchange Board of India (SEBI): In 1992, the Capital Issues (Control) Act, 1947 was repealed and the office of the Controller of Capital Issues (CCIs) was abolished. SEBI was set up in April 1988 by an administrative order and acquired a statutory status in 1992. With this ended all controls related to raising of funds from the market. Issuers of capital, however, are required to meet the guidelines of SEBI on disclosures and protection of investors. The move was aimed at enhancing the efficiency, safety, integrity and transparency of the market.

SEBI has emerged as an autonomous and independent statutory body with a definite mandate which requires it to: (a) protect the interest of the investors in securities, (b) promote the development of the securities market, and (c) regulate the securities market.

The SEBI prohibits fraudulent and unfair trade practices, including insider trading. It also regulates substantial acquisition of shares and takeovers. In order to ensure protection of investors and to safeguard the integrity of the markets, there is a comprehensive surveillance system. Stock exchanges are the primary targets for detection of market manipulation, price rigging and other regulatory breaches regarding capital market functioning.

In order to achieve these objectives, SEBI exercises powers under: (a) SEBI Act, (b) Securities Contracts (Regulation) Act, (c) Depositories Act, and (d) delegated powers under the Companies Act.

SEBI regulates and supervises the securities market through its various regulations, guidelines and schemes issued from time to time.

Securitisation: See Asset Securitisation, *8*.

Securitisation, Reconstruction of Financial Assets and Enforcement of Security Interest (SARFAESI) Act, 2002: The enactment of SARFAESI Act, 2002 was an important landmark in the ongoing reforms in the financial sector. The Act enables the setting up of asset management companies, addressing the problem of non-performing assets (NPAs) of banks and financial institutions and enhancing creditor rights. The main provisions of the Act are as follows.

1. A securitisation company or reconstruction company having own funds of not less than ₹ 2 crore or such other amount not exceeding 15 percent of total financial assets acquired or to be acquired as specified by the RBI can commence business after obtaining a certificate of registration, subject to fulfilling certain conditions and complying with the prudential norms set by the RBI.
2. The securitisation or reconstruction company may acquire assets of any bank or financial institution by issuing a debenture or bond or any other security for consideration agreed upon between such company and the bank or the financial institution.
3. Notice of acquisition of a financial asset may be sent by bank or financial institution to an obligor. The obligor on receipt of such notice will make payment to the securitisation company concerned.
4. A securitisation company may raise funds from qualified institutional buyers by formulating schemes for acquiring financial assets.
5. In the event of non-realisation of financial assets, qualified institutional buyers of a securitisation company holding not less than 75 percent of the total value of securities issued by such company are entitled to call for a meeting of all institutional buyers and the resolution passed in such a meeting is binding on the company.
6. A securitisation or a reconstruction company may provide for the proper management of the business of the borrower, sale or lease of a part or whole of the business of borrower, settlement of dues payable by the borrower and taking possession of secured assets within the framework of guidelines framed by the RBI.
7. Other functions of the securitisation company include acting as an agent for any bank or financial institution for the purpose of recovery of their dues.
8. Secured creditor is entitled to enforce any security interest created in its favour without the intervention of the court or tribunal.

9. In case of non-performing debts, the secured creditor is entitled to serve a notice to the borrower to discharge his liabilities within 60 days.
10. In case of failure to discharge the liabilities in the stipulated period, the secured creditor is entitled to take possession of secured assets, take over the management of secured assets and to appoint any person to manage the same.
11. Borrowers are entitled to prefer an appeal with the Debts Recovery Tribunal after depositing 75 percent of the amount claimed by the secured creditor. Borrowers aggrieved by the order of the Debts Recovery Tribunal may prefer an appeal to an Appellate Tribunal within 30 days from the date of receipt of the order of Debts Recovery Tribunal.

Settlement Advisory Committees have also been formed at regional and head office levels of commercial banks. Furthermore, banks can also issue notices under the SARFAESI Act, 2002 for enforcement of security interest without intervention of courts. Thus, banks have a menu of options to resolve their problem of NPAs.

With a view to providing an additional option and developing a healthy secondary market for NPAs, guidelines on sale/purchase of non-performing assets were issued in July 2005 where securitisation companies and reconstruction companies are not involved. The draft guidelines cover the following broad areas: (a) procedure for purchase/sale of non-performing financial assets by banks, including valuation and pricing aspects, and (b) prudential norms relating to asset classification, provisioning, accounting of recoveries, capital adequacy and exposure norms and disclosure requirements.

The RBI and the Central Government have initiated several institutional measures to contain the levels of NPAs, including the following.

1. Corporate Debt Restructuring (q.v.).
2. Debt Recovery Tribunals (q.v.).
3. *Lok Adalats* (q.v.).

Self-Assessment: It is a system of income tax under which the taxpayer is required to declare his taxable income, submit a calculation of the tax due from him, and make the payment of the amount he regards as due. Tax authorities check in a sample of cases the correctness of income disclosed, exemptions and deductions claimed, and calculation of tax amount. This system is different from the one under which tax administration is itself responsible for establishing the tax due and demanding payment.

Self-help Group (SHG): A self-help group (SHG) is a small voluntary association of 10-20 poor people from the same socio-economic background who come together for the purpose of addressing their common socio-economic problems through self-help and mutual-help. They collect small savings (thrift) on regular basis. Out of the pooled money, small interest bearing loans are given to the members and some amount is deposited with a bank regularly. The bank lends money for economic activities of the group without collateral security and at market rates. The savings of poor members are pooled resources saved with great difficulty. This hard-earned money is termed as *warm money.* The money obtained by the group from outsiders, i.e. banks, micro finance institutions is termed as *cold money.*

Members make small regular contributions over a few months until there is enough capital with the group to begin lending. Funds may then be lent back to the members or to others in the village for any purpose. In India, many SHGs are *linked* to banks for the delivery of micro credit.

SHGs are started by non-governmental organizations (NGOs) that generally have broad anti-poverty agendas. SHGs are seen as instruments for a variety of goals including empowering women, developing leadership abilities among poor people, increasing school enrolments, and improving nutrition and the use of birth control. Financial intermediation is generally seen more as an entry point to these other goals, rather than as a primary objective.

SHGs have been instrumental in initiating micro entrepreneurial activities among those poor people who have been neglected so far and far away from the process of social as well economic development. Self-help groups-bank linkage programme is responsible for developing banking habits among the poorest of the poor people.

The basic objective of self-help group is upliftment of poor people by means of micro economic activities so that the members get job opportunities, sustainable income and some assets for generation of regular income. There is tremendous enthusiasm in formation of the groups but care is not taken for their proper growth and survival.

The most significant contribution of SHGs is that they have been instrumental in building up enough confidence among the poor people and now they are ready to participate in the process of development. Many of these have been running fair price shops very successfully. A sizable number of the groups are working as caterers for the State Government-sponsored mid-day meal scheme. It is noteworthy that a good number of the SHGs have been marketing successfully the products of domestic as well as multinational corporations in remote rural areas.

Service Charge: A charge assessed by a depository institution for processing transactions and maintaining accounts.

Share Transfer: It is a transaction for the ownership of shares. A share transfer form is completed by the seller and sent with the share certificate to the company's registered office. The buyer's name is then entered in the share register. The buyer bears the cost of registration, duty on the shares and brokerage.

Signature Card: A card signed by each depositor and customer of a bank which may be used as a means of identification. The signature card represents a contract between the bank and the depositor.

Sinking Fund: It refers to a fund to which a debtor makes periodic contributions to facilitate retirement of a debt.

Small Industries Development Bank of India (SIDBI): Set up in 1990, SIDBI is a wholly owned subsidiary of Industrial Development Bank of India (IDBI). It was established for the promotion, financing and development of industry in the small scale, tiny and cottage sector. It acts as the chief refinancing institution in this sector.

Sniffing: It involves the use of a software programme that is illicitly inserted somewhere on a network to capture ("sniff") user passwords as they pass through the system.

Soft Loan: It is a loan from a government or multilateral development bank with a long repayment period and below-the-market interest rate.

South Asian Association for Regional Co-operation (SAARC): On December 8, 1985, the seven South Asian States, viz. India, Pakistan, Nepal, Bangladesh, Bhutan, Sri Lanka, and Maldives formally launched the South Asian Association for Regional Cooperation (SAARC). Broadly speaking, SAARC countries comprise the Indian sub-continent, an area which was usually referred to, prior to 1947, as Britain's Indian empire. Sharing a common colonial legacy of socio-economic backwardness, they inhabit one-fifth of world population and face the twin formidable problems of unemployment and poverty. At the same time, these countries provide a vast investment and market potential in a basically free enterprise environment. SAARC, with its headquarters located in Kathmandu, Nepal, is an example of south-south co-operation.

The underlying objective of this regional grouping is to strive for co-operative efforts to accelerate the economic development of this region, one of the poorest in the world. This institutional arrangement is intended to provide scope for discussing bilateral issues and exploring areas for co-operative linkages in socio-economic field. SAARC charter pledges non-interference by members in each others internal affairs. Under its rules, all decisions are to be unanimous and no tendentious issues can be brought before this forum. This is one hope for the smooth and expanding co-operation among the member countries despite their different systems of governance. Areas identified for mutual co-operation range from agriculture, forestry, health and population, science and technology, art and culture and curbing terrorism.

Special Drawing Rights (SDRs): These were created as a new and additional form of international reserves/liquidity in 1970 under the International Monetary Fund (IMF). Under this scheme, countries receive SDRs as per their share in reserve assets and have an automatic right to draw them from IMF over and above other drawing facilities. SDRs constitute a permanent net addition to international liquidity.

A deficit country uses SDRs for settling deficit by exchanging SDRs for whatever currency it requires. Other countries accept SDRs as gold or convertible currencies. Its value is based on the values of a *standard basket* of five major currencies. Thus, SDRs are like monetary gold or assets that have no corresponding liability. In balance of payments, allocation of SDRs (credit) forms the counterpart that matches the rise (debit) in a country's holding of SDRs which form the part of reserves. Most central banks include SDRs as assets.

It was in 1967 that the Board of Governors of the IMF agreed at the annual meetings in Rio de Janeiro to create a new international monetary reserve asset to be named the special drawing right. SDRs can be created only by the IMF. The legal framework for their creation and allocation to member countries was established by the first amendment to the Articles of Agreement of the IMF adopted in 1968. The second amendment (1978) provided for a considerable liberalisation of the rules governing the use of the SDRs. On January 1, 1970, the first distribution of 3.4 billion SDRs was made to IMF member countries followed by subsequent distributions.

Special Economic Zones (SEZs): SEZs are geographical regions in a country that have economic laws that are more liberal than typical economic laws of that country. The word *special* mainly means special economic system and policies. A SEZ can be deemed as a *foreign territory* for the purposes of trade operations, duties and tariffs. Units in SEZs enjoy lot of fiscal pampering.

SEZs are self-contained islands providing high-quality infrastructural facilities. SEZs offer industrial, residential and commercial areas with developed plots/pre-built factories, power, telecommunications, water supply, sewerage and drainage, and educational and medical facilities.

SEZs have been established in several countries, including China, India, Iran, Jordan, Poland, Kazakhstan, Philippines and Russia. SEZs are known by different names in different countries. Some close variants of SEZs are growth centres, industrial estates, export zones, industrial parks etc. In the United States, SEZ are referred to as *Urban Enterprise Zones*.

Specific Duty: A specific or volumetric duty represents a fixed amount of tax on a unit of the physical quantity of the product. Customs duties, excise levies, and sales taxes on commodities may take specific or *ad valorem* form.

Specific duty is generally preferred for commodities the classifications and sub-classifications of which are not numerous, i.e. the commodity is a standardised one, e.g. sugar. A specific duty is easy to apply besides having the political and psychological advantages of obscuring the actual ratio of the tax to the selling price. It is, however, price-neutral in the sense that price changes, if any, in the commodity do not affect the revenue yield. Specific duty is quality-neutral also unless differential rates are prescribed with reference to the quality of the product.

There can be many variants of the specific form of duty. If a flat amount per unit of a commodity is levied irrespective of the price range, it is a simple specific duty. It may be simple specific with initial exemption. However, if the flat amount per unit changes with the price range of the commodity, it becomes a graduated specific duty. See also *Ad Valorem* Duty.

Spoofing: It refers to an attempt to gain access to a system by posing as an authorised user.

Spot Deal: It is a deal for a currency for delivery within two business days. It is also known as value spot.

Spread: It is the difference between the buying and selling prices of a currency.

Square Position: When sales and purchases of a currency are equal, it is known as a square position. It is also called *square book, flat book* or *matched book.*

Statement: A summary of all transactions that occurred over the preceding month and could be associated with a deposit account or a credit card account.

Statutory Liquidity Ratio (SLR): See Reserve Bank of India, *191*.

Stock Exchange: An organised market for the buying and selling of stocks and bonds. Stock exchanges provide facilities for secondary market, i.e. transactions in existing securities. People desirous of converting their cash into securities can go to the stock exchange and buy securities through brokers. Similarly, securities can be converted into cash by selling them in the market. Transactions in the secondary market reflect investment climate in the economy.

Stock Market: A stock (or share) market deals mainly in corporate securities like shares and debentures. The purpose of these securities is to raise long-term funds for companies engaged in production. Thus, stock market is an important component of the capital market of the financial system. Function of the stock market is two-fold: (a) to arrange for the raising of new capital (primary market function), and (b) to provide liquidity to existing securities (secondary market function). New capital is raised by the issue of shares and debentures.

Corporate enterprises raising new capital may be new companies or existing companies planning expansion of their operations. Sometimes, existing private firms *go public*, i.e. become public limited companies. Stock market helps the floatation of new issue by providing a variety of services like underwriting, distribution and listing of the issue. Underwriting means guaranteeing the purchase of a fixed amount of new issue by the underwriter. The new issue of capital may be a public issue or a right issue or both in certain proportions. It may be in the form of equity shares or debentures. Debentures, in turn, may be fully convertible, partly convertible or non-convertible into shares. A public issue means the general public is invited to subscribe to the new issue. A right issue is restricted for subscription by existing shareholders of the company.

Stocks and Flows: Both stocks and flows are variables or quantities. Flows have time dimension, i.e. they are measured over a period of time. Conversely, stocks are measured at a particular point of time. Like a balance sheet, a stock position has a reference to a particular date and shows position on that date. A flow shows change during a period of time. Thus, national income is a flow variable because it describes and measures the flow of goods and services which become available to a country during a year. Contrarily, national capital is a stock variable which shows, on a particular date, the stock of machines, plants, buildings etc. owned by a country. In short, all economic variables which are related to a period of time are called flow variables, e.g. income, expenditure, savings, depreciation and change in inventories. Conversely, all economic variables which are related to a point of time are known as stock variables, e.g. capital, wealth and foreign debt. Stock and flow variables are interrelated. Thus, increase in national income increases national capital and increase in national capital generates larger national income.

Stop Payment: An order not to pay a cheque that has been issued but not yet cashed. If requested soon enough, the cheque will not be debited from the payer's account. Most banks charge a fee for this service.

Straight-line Depreciation Method: Under this method, the historic cost of the depreciating asset is apportioned in equal amounts for deduction over the period of its estimated economic life which is normally specified in the tax law for each group of assets. Thus, if a machine is purchased for ₹ 50,000 and the tax law specifies that this asset can be written off at a rate of 20 percent, then the yearly depreciation deduction will be ₹ 10,000 for 5 years.

Strategic Risk: Strategic risk is one of the most significant risks for banking organisations. Strategic risk differs from other risk categories in that it is more general and broad in nature. Strategic decisions taken by a bank will have implications for all other risk categories.

Subsidies: A subsidy is a grant of money from an outside third party to either the buyer or the seller of a commodity. Subsidies allow a buyer to procure a commodity/service at a lower price than would otherwise have been necessary. Similarly, a business firm will not stay in operation unless revenue is sufficient enough to cover cost plus some return on investment. If revenue from buyers is insufficient, a subsidy from an outside agency may keep the firm in operation.

The effect of a subsidy is opposite of the effect of a tax. A cash subsidy is the opposite of a direct tax while a subsidised commodity is the opposite of a taxed commodity. Hence, subsidies are sometimes called negative taxation.

Surcharge: It is an additional tax calculated on the normal tax liability. In other words, surcharge is assessed on the usual amount of tax due.

Swaps: Swaps take many forms but often entail the exchange of one type of asset or payment for another.

- **Currency swaps** convert principal from the lender's currency into the debtor's currency and receiving interest payments in the debtor's currency.
- **Debt swaps** entail replacing the foreign liabilities of a debtor country with ownership or rights of value.
- **Debt-for-equity swap** replaces foreign liabilities with a stake in the debtor country's national enterprises.
- **Debt-for-export swap** replaces foreign liabilities with an arrangement to receive proceeds from the overseas sale of the debtor country's products or commodities.
- **Debt-for-debt swap** replaces an existing foreign liability with a new commitment from the debtor country.
- **Interest rate swaps** involve agreements on the means for exchanging future cash flows.
- **Single currency interest rate swaps** concern exchanging future cash flow in the same currency and offer a means for modifying the impact of future changes in interest rates on a company's profitability.
- **Cross currency interest rate swaps** concern exchanging future cash flows between one currency and another, traded either on a fixed or floating rate, and offer a means for limited the risk of converting financial interests between currencies.

The swap, made to protect the principal from future changes in foreign exchange rates, involves a forward exchange contract to recover the currency involved. Swaps also involve arrangements whereby different sellers of similar commodities swap and deliver them to each other's customer if such action saves transportation costs. See also Credit Derivatives, and Financial Derivatives.

Tt

Tangible Asset: See Asset, *8*.

Tariff: It is a tax assessed by a government in accordance with its tariff schedule on goods as they enter (or leave) a country. It may be imposed to protect domestic industries from imported goods and/or to generate revenue.

Tax: A tax is a compulsory payment made to general government without any direct *quid pro quo*. General government includes central, state and local governments. Tax payments are compulsory and the benefits provided by government to taxpayers are neither direct nor proportional to such payments. Every tax is made up of two elements: a base, i.e. the object to be taxed, and a rate structure indicating how the base is to be taxed.

Tax Amnesty: It is an opportunity offered by a government to tax evaders to declare their past concealment of income, wealth etc., without fear of being prosecuted. Tax amnesty (or impunity) is granted only for the past in order to secure better compliance and higher tax yield in the present and future. A tax amnesty brings concealed money in the open, broadens the base of investment, and hence accelerates economic development. However, tax amnesties set bad precedents and encourage tax evaders in the hope that they will be let off leniently for their past sins any time in the future. Practically, the same group of tax evaders takes advantage of tax amnesties announced by a government. The honest taxpayers are demoralised and the tax enforcement machinery also loses respect in the eyes of the common man.

Tax Evasion: It is an illegal attempt to reduce tax payable through deliberate under-reporting/non-reporting taxable incomes or concealing one's true *state of affairs* from tax authorities. Tax evasion is a criminal offence and if detected is punishable by financial penalties or even by imprisonment or both.

Tax Holiday: It is a tax incentive targeted at new firms, and is not available to existing units. Under a tax holiday scheme, new enterprises are allowed a period of time free from the burden of income tax, subject to certain conditions.

Term Draft: It is a bill of exchange payable at a fixed or determinable future time.

Terms: The period of time and the interest rate arranged between creditor and debtor to repay a loan.

Thin Market: The term refers to a relatively inactive market with a low-volume, low-value turnover.

Through Bill of Lading: See Bill of Lading, *22*.

Tied Aid Credit: Tied aid credit refers to the practice of providing grants and/or concessional loans, either alone or combined with export credits, linked to procurement from the donor country.

Tied Loan: It is a loan made by a government agency that requires a foreign borrower to spend the proceeds in the lender's country or to buy the lender's products.

Time Deposit: A time deposit (also known as a term deposit) is a money deposit at a bank that cannot be withdrawn for a certain *term* or period of time. When the term is over it can be withdrawn, or it can be held for another term. The longer the term, the better the yield on the money. Generally, there are significant penalties for early withdrawal.

Total Return Swap (TRS): See Credit Derivatives, *47*.

Trade Cycles: See Business Cycles, *29*.

Transactor Principle: There are two principles that may serve as the basis for geographic allocation of financial flows: the debtor/creditor principle and the transactor principle. Under the transactor principle, transactions resulting from changes in the claims and liabilities are allocated to the country of residence of the non-resident party to the transaction (the transactor), even if this is not the country of residence of the direct investment enterprise or direct investor. See also Debtor/Creditor Principle.

Transfer Pricing: It is that price at which a parent firm (MNC) sells its product/technology to its subsidiaries in other countries. Alternatively, it refers to the price attached to transactions between the divisions (e.g. branches or subsidiaries) of a company. Transfer pricing is usually considered in a global context, particularly in relation to cross-frontier transactions within a multinational company.

Determination of transfer price has significance in relation to such matters as taxation, exchange restrictions, and currency fluctuations. The incentive for transfer price manipulations is provided by varying rates of taxation in countries where a multinational company operates. Thus, where goods are being transferred from a company in a low tax country to a subsidiary company in a high tax country, there is a clear tax incentive if a high transfer price is ensured to maximise profit within the low tax country.

Similarly, sales of a multinational group may be routed through a specially formed tax haven distribution company. The tax haven company purchases goods from affiliated companies at the lowest possible prices and sells to independent purchasers at the full market price, ensuring that most or all of the profit from the transaction is earned in the tax haven.

Due to the inherent difficulties in determining a fair or market price for inter-company transactions, a multinational company has always the option to fix artificial transfer prices.

Transnational Corporation: It is a company which operates in a home country and has an affiliate overseas. The terms transnational corporation and multinational corporation are now used synonymously.

Trust Receipt: Release of merchandise by a bank to a buyer in which the bank retains title to the merchandise. The buyer, who obtains the goods for manufacturing or sales purposes, is obligated to maintain the goods (or the proceeds from their sale) distinct from the remainder of his/her assets and to hold them ready for repossession by the bank.

Uu

Ultimate Consignee: The ultimate consignee is the person located abroad who is the true party in interest, receiving the export for the designated end-use.

Uncollected Funds: A portion of a deposit balance that has not yet been collected by the depository bank.

Undistributed Profits Tax: It is imposed on companies which allow their retained profits to accumulate beyond the reasonable needs of business. Companies may prefer to hold profits rather than pay dividends so that their shareholders could postpone personal income taxes that would have to be paid if the dividends were paid out. The undistributed profits tax attempts to checkmate this practice on the part of companies.

Unit Tax: See Specific Duty, *211*.

Unit Trust of India (UTI): Set up in 1964, it reflected the efforts of the Government of India to popularise unit trusts and mutual funds in the country to encourage indirect holding of securities by the public. The UTI was established to mobilise the savings of the small investors who constitute the bulk of India's population. Government has extended various types of concessions including tax benefits to UTI and its unit holders. The UTI with a large investor base, has been running various schemes including the flagship, US-64, various assured returns schemes, and other NAV-based schemes.

Recently, important decisions have been taken to tide over the financial problems faced by the UTI. On October 28, 2002, an ordinance was promulgated which repealed the UTI Act, and created two entities, UTI-1 and UTI-2. UTI-2 is an unencumbered mutual fund, with only NAV-based schemes. UTI-1 has US-64 and the assured returns schemes. On 15 January 2003, the handover of UTI-2 to a new set of owners (State Bank of India, Bank of Baroda, Punjab National Bank and Life Insurance Corporation of India) took place.

Unsecured Loan: It is a loan which is not secured on any property/assets. Contrarily, a secured loan/debt is guaranteed by assets.

Urban Co-operative Banks (UCBs): The co-operative banking system forms an integral part of the Indian financial system. It comprises urban cooperative banks and rural co-operative credit institutions. Urban co-operative banks have a single-tier structure whereas rural co-operatives have a two- or three-tier structure.

The single tier urban co-operative banks (UCBs)—also referred to as primary cooperative banks—play an important role in meeting the growing credit needs of urban and semi-urban areas of the country. The UCBs, which grew rapidly in the early 1990s, showed certain weaknesses arising out of lack of sound corporate governance, unethical lending, comparatively high levels of non-performing loans and their inability to operate in a liberalised environment. Accordingly, some of the weak UCBs have been either liquidated or merged with other banks.

Co-operative banks in India are more than 100 years old. These banks came into existence with the enactment of the Agricultural Credit Co-operative Societies Act in 1904. Co-operative banks form an integral part of the banking system in India. These banks operate mainly for the benefit of rural areas, particularly the agricultural sector. Co-operative banks mobilise deposits and supply agricultural and rural credit with a wider outreach. They are the main source of institutional credit to the farmers. Co-operative banks are chiefly responsible for breaking the monopoly of moneylenders in providing credit to agriculturists. They have also been an important instrument for various development schemes, particularly subsidy-based programmes for the poor. Co-operative banks operate for non-agricultural sector also but their role is small.

Though much smaller as compared to scheduled commercial

banks, co-operative banks constitute an important segment of the Indian banking system. They have an extensive branch network and reach out to people in remote areas. They have traditionally played an important role in creating banking habits among the lower and middle-income groups and in strengthening the rural credit delivery system.

Urban co-operative banks play an important role in meeting the growing credit needs of urban and semi-urban areas. UCBs mobilise savings from the middle and lower income groups and purvey credit to small borrowers, including weaker sections of the society. Scheduled UCBs are under closer regulatory and supervisory framework of the RBI.

The financial reforms process initiated in 1991 has tried to achieve regulatory convergence among various financial intermediaries in view of their systemic importance. Therefore, the basic objectives and instruments of reforms for co-operative banks have been the same as for State Co-operative Banks (SCBs). However, given the special characteristics of co-operative banks, they have been extended certain dispensations in terms of pace and sequencing of reforms.

UCBs have grown rapidly since the early 1990s. During the phase of rapid expansion, however, the sector showed certain weaknesses arising out of: (a) lack of sound corporate governance, (b) unethical lending, (c) comparatively high level of loan defaults, and (d) inability to operate in a liberalised and competitive environment. The RBI, therefore, has been striving to harness the growth of UCBs with appropriate application of prudential regulation and supervision to safeguard the interests of depositors. Keeping in view the weak financial position of many UCBs, the RBI has undertaken a series of measures directed towards strengthening of the UCBs. Since March 31, 1993, the UCBs have been advised to adhere to the prudential norms which include, *inter alia*, the following.

1. Applying capital adequacy standards.
2. Prescribing an asset-liability management framework.
3. Enhancing the proportion of holding of Government and other

approved securities for the purpose of statutory liquidity ratio (SLR) stipulation.

4. Restriction on bank finance against the security of corporate shares and debentures.
5. Limiting the exposure to capital market investment.

In view of the challenges arising from the functioning of the UCBs for the financial system, the RBI appointed a High Power Committee (Chairman: K. Madhava Rao), 1999 to review the performance of UCBs and to suggest necessary measures to strengthen this sector. Based on the recommendations of this Committee, measures have been initiated to strengthen the existing urban banking structure.

User Charge: A fee or charge for use of a government-supplied service, generally transportation service. It is applied so that those who benefit from public transport services repay the cost to the government. User charges are usually in the form of tolls, licence fees, and fuel taxes and fall on highway and waterway traffic.

There are three categories of user charges: (a) service fees levied for performing specific services, e.g. registration of animals, vehicles etc. These are collected from identifiable individuals and are in the nature of cost reimbursement from the private to the government sector, (b) public prices paid voluntarily by identifiable private individuals through the purchase of publicly-provided private goods and services by government agencies, and (c) specific benefit taxes are compulsory payments related in some ways to benefits received by taxpayers, e.g. land value increment levies, and fuel taxes on road users.

Usury: Charging an illegally high interest rate on a loan.

Usury Rates: The maximum rate of interest lenders may charge borrowers. The usury rate is generally set by law.

UTI: See Unit Trust of India, *220*.

Vv

Valorisation: It is a system under which the cost of public works is allocated to the beneficiary properties in proportion to the estimated benefits conferred on them by those works.

Valuation of Stocks: It means using market price as the basis for valuation. However, it is recognised that, in practice, book values from the balance sheets of direct investment enterprises (or investors) are often used to determine the value of the stock of direct investment.

Value Added Tax (VAT): Value added tax is levied on the sellers of goods and services based on value added by their respective units. The base of VAT is determined by value added at a particular stage of production or distribution. Meaning of VAT becomes clearer when it is juxtaposed against conventional turnover tax (excise duty, sales tax) which falls on the total value of the product at each stage of production chain and is called a *cascade* type tax. VAT, a fiscal innovation of early 1960s, has claimed world-wide attention as more and more countries are adopting it in varying degrees to reform their system of commodity taxation.

Variable Rate: Any interest rate or dividend that changes on a periodic basis.

VAT: See Value Added Tax, *224*.

Vehicle Currency: It refers to that currency which acts as a medium of exchange in the foreign exchange market as, for example, US dollar. Exchange rate between two currencies is often determined through it.

Veil of Money: According to this concept, money is merely a medium of exchange and hence neutral. Behind the money transactions lies the real process, i.e. exchange of goods for goods. People often fail to see through the veil of money and consider money as having value in itself. See also Money Illusion.

Venture Capital: It is a term used for investment made in those lines where risk element is very high, especially in new lines of production, new markets or new processes.

Volumetric Duty: See Specific Duty, *211*.

Voluntary Bankruptcy: See Bankruptcy, *16*.

Vostro Account: A foreign bank's account with a local bank is called vostro account. For example, rupee account of a New York bank with a Mumbai bank is a vostro account as far as Mumbai bank is concerned. See also Nostro Account.

Voting Stocks: These are equity/shares that give voting rights to the holder. These can either be listed voting stocks (i.e. equity/shares that are listed on an official stock exchange) or unlisted voting stock (i.e. equity/shares that are not listed on an official stock exchange).

Ww

Warranty: It attests the supplier's commitment to quality and after-sale services (maintenance facilities, spare parts etc.). This is an increasingly important tool in international business these days.

Ways and Means Advances: These are short-term loans (also called floating debt) made by the central bank of a country to the government of that country. The purpose of ways and means advances is to accommodate temporary mismatch in the receipts and payments of the government.

Wealth Tax: Wealth represents the command a person has over economic resources at any point of time. Tax base for purposes of wealth tax is normally the taxpayer's net wealth i.e. total assets less liabilities. The base is generally modified by exemptions and deductions. The tax may be imposed on companies or individuals or both. Similarly, the tax may be imposed at either a flat rate or at a progressive rate.

Wealth tax is advocated on both benefit and ability-to-pay considerations. Protection of life and property has traditionally been a primary function of the government and to perform the same, considerable cost is incurred on law enforcement machinery and judicial administration. The main beneficiaries of these services are the people with fabulous wealth who, as a rule, should contribute towards the expenses on such services. Pavement sleepers hardly need the services of the state as protector of property. Another dimension of the benefit argument is that public services like roads, street lighting, community centres, public parks etc., increase the value of real estates, conferring unearned benefits on the owners of such estates. Therefore, it can be argued that property owners should pay for these services.

Withholding Tax: A system of collecting income tax whereby money is periodically deducted by the employers, financial institutions, and others from wages of employees, returns on securities, and other payments. Thus, intermediaries (or third parties) do the job on behalf of the government as regards assessment of the taxable base and the collection of tax thereon.

Generally, a fixed percentage is withheld from the payment made and the same is deposited in the government's account. At the time of filing the return of income, the taxpayer encloses withholding tax receipts, and in case of overpayment can claim refund of tax.

Tax withholding system (also called tax deduction at source or Pay-As-You-Earn) satisfies the canon of convenience both for the fiscal authorities and the taxpayers. It is beneficial for the government because it reduces the possibility of tax evasion, ensures prompt tax payment, and simplifies tax collection. It does not allow any lag between the time of receiving income and the time of tax payment. For the taxpayer, it is an instalment plan of taxation and hence convenient.

However, tax withholding involves additional paper work on the part of tax deductors. It also adds to the burden of taxpayers who have to obtain tax deduction certificates from deductors, fill additional tax forms, and wait for refunds. See also Advance Tax Payment.

World Bank: The World Bank is an integrated group of international institutions which provides financial and technical assistance to developing countries. The World Bank includes the International Bank for Reconstruction and Development and the International Development Association. World Bank affiliates, legally and financially separate, include the International Centre for Settlement of Investment Disputes, the International Finance Corporation, and the Multilateral Investment Guarantee Agency. World Bank headquarters are in Washington DC.

International Bank for Reconstruction and Development IBRD): IBRD started functioning in 1946 as one of the two international institutions agreed to at the Bretton Woods

Conference of July 1944. The other Bretton Woods institution is the International Monetary Fund. During the negotiations which preceded the Bretton Woods Conference, the British, led by John Maynard Keynes (1883-1946), favoured a single organisation, an International Clearing Union to manage the world money so as to reduce international economic fluctuations as well as the fluctuations in the balance of payments of member countries. Negotiators from the US preferred two organisations, a bank for long-term lending and a fund for short-term lending. The proposals of the US were ultimately accepted.

To begin with, the Bank was asked to assist the external financing of the reconstruction of Europe at the conclusion of World War II. However, it was soon realised that the resources of the Bank were too few and its organisation too new for this task. In the initial years of Bank's functioning, lending operations remained scanty for purposes of development. This low level of lending was due to its small lending capacity, its conservative management and the unsettled state of knowledge concerning the development process. Bank's financing was largely confined to large infrastructure projects, such as transportation networks, and it was criticised for being too cautious with the development needs of its poor members.

International Finance Corporation (IFC): It is a subsidiary of World Bank created in 1956 to invest funds in private enterprises without government guarantees.

International Development Association (IDA): In 1960, a third organisation, IDA was created to offer loans to low-income member countries on soft terms and conditions. This soft or concessionary assistance is made possible by contributions to the IDA by the governments of high-income countries. The management of the Bank is thus enabled to offer rates of interest and loan maturities which take into account the nature of the projects financed and the ability of borrowing governments to service the debt. The IDA is financed by periodic government contributions. The Bank obtains the funds it lends from the paid-in portion of the subscriptions of member governments and from earnings on past loans. Member governments of the Bank are represented by governors who meet periodically to receive the annual report of the officers of the Bank and to conduct necessary business. Governors and executive directors vote in accordance with the voting power of the governments they represent. Voting power is related to the subscriptions of the member governments and is based on a formula which takes into account such factors as gross national product and volume of foreign trade.

Presently, the Bank is the world's leading inter-governmental organisation engaged in the external financing of economic development in less developed countries. Loans given by the Bank help to finance the imports needed to complete approved development projects. Its advice helps to determine the priorities, the scale and the nature of the projects financed by it and through the development assistance programmes of industrial countries, by private banks, regional development banks and sources internal to the developing countries themselves. While the Bank is a wholly independent international organisation operating under its own Articles of Agreement, the staff of the bank co-ordinates its work with the relevant agencies of the United Nations and other international bodies.

World Trade Organization (WTO): WTO is the only international body dealing with the rules of trade between nations. At its heart are the WTO agreements, the legal ground rules for international commerce and for trade policy. The agreements have three main objectives: (a) to help trade flow as freely as possible, (b) to achieve further liberalisation gradually through negotiations and (c) to set up an impartial means of settling disputes.

Written Down Value: It is the value of a depreciable asset determined by deducting from the actual cost the depreciation allowances granted by income tax authorities in previous tax years. Actual cost – Depreciation = Written down value

WTO: See World Trade Organization, *229*.

Xx, Yy and Zz

X-efficiency: The concept of X-efficiency, attributed to Harvey Leibenstein, is an important issue in economic development. It is basically concerned about why people do not work as hard or as effectively as they could. In other words, X-efficiency deals with how human inputs affect economic development. X-efficiency is generally contrasted with allocative (or static) efficiency.

York-Antwerp Rules: They refer to an international set of regulations governing maritime shipping designed to help settle disputes arising from losses. They often are incorporated in shipping contracts.

Zero-bracket Income: It is that amount of taxable income which is taxed at a rate of zero percent. Under the Indian Income Tax Act, 1961, the first slice of income of ₹ 2 lakh of a general category individual is taxed at zero percent (financial year 2013-14). It is also called basic exemption.

Zero-rated Goods: Under Value Added Tax (q.v.), there are sometimes zero-rated goods like food, newspapers and medical prescriptions. For such goods, no VAT is charged on output but VAT suffered on inputs is reclaimable. Hence, zero-rated goods escape entirely from VAT. On the other hand, there are services like postage, education, and health which are exempt from VAT. No VAT is charged on these services but no VAT can be reclaimed on inputs. Hence, exempt goods do not suffer any tax on the value added at the final stage.

Zero-tax Company: Income tax laws usually provide for a host of deductions and incentives to promote socio-economic objectives of state policy. It is likely that a profit-making company may arrange its affairs in such a way that the cumulative effect of all deductions is to reduce its income declared in the tax return to zero. To deal with such situations, some countries have introduced Minimum Alternative Tax (q.v.).

Glossary of E-money and E-banking Terms

Access Products: Products which allow consumers to access traditional payment instruments electronically, generally from remote locations.

Applet: A small application programme that is designed to do a small, specific job.

Application: A computer programme or set of programmes that perform the processing of records for a specific function.

Asynchronous Transfer Mode (ATM): Method of transmitting bits of data one after another with a start bit and a stop bit to mark the beginning and end of each data unit.

Auditability: The degree to which transactions can be traced and audited through a system.

Authentication: The process of proving the claimed identity of an individual user, machine, software component or any other entity.

Authorization: The process of determining what types of activities are permitted. Usually, authorization is in the context of authentication: once you have authenticated a user, they may be authorized different types of access or activity.

Bandwidth: The transmission capacity of a computer channel or communications line.

Bastion Host: A system that has been hardened to resist attack, and which is installed on a network in such a way that it is expected to potentially come under attack. Bastion hosts are often components of firewalls, or may be *outside* web servers or public access systems.

Biometrics: A method of verifying an individual's identity by analyzing a unique physical attribute.

Browser: A computer programme that enables the user to retrieve information that has been made publicly available on the Internet; also permits multimedia (graphics) applications on the World Wide Web.

Byte: Fixed number of binary digits, often representing a single character.

CD-ROM: Compact Disk-Read on Memory.

Chip Card: Also known as an integrated circuit (IC) card, it is a card containing one or more computer chips or integrated circuits for identification, data storage or special-purpose processing used to validate personal identification numbers, authorize purchases, verify account balances and store personal records.

Chip: An electronic device consisting of circuit elements on a single silicon chip. The most complex circuits are microprocessors, which are single chips that contain the complete arithmetic and logic units of computers.

Client-Server Network: A method of allocating resources in a local area network so that computing power is distributed among computer workstations in the network but some shared resources are centralized in a file server.

Closed Network: A telecommunications network that is used for a specific purpose, such as a payment system, and to which access is restricted (also referred to as a private network).

Closed Stored Value System: A system in which value is issued and accepted by either a relatively small group of merchants, or in which the system is limited geographically (i.e. university programmes and fare cards for mass transit systems).

Code: Computer programmes written in machine language (object code) or programming language (source code).

CPU: Central Processing Unit.

Cracker: A computer operator who breaks through a system's security. This can be legitimate activity, such as to test system security measures.

Cryptography: The principles, means, and methods for rendering information unintelligible and for restoring encrypted information to intelligible form (i.e. scrambling a message).

Cursor: Movable dot on the computer screen which indicates a particular position.

Cyber Mall: A set of electronic or digital storefronts linked through a common web site.

Data Mining: It refers to the practice of using algorithms to find patterns in customer transaction data to market specific products and services to customers.

Data Warehouse: A data warehouse is a large database of customer transactions, updated regularly, which is used as a source of information for data mining.

Database Administrator (DBA): The individual with authority to control the data base management system.

Denial of Service: A denial of service attack represents an attempt to overwhelm a server with requests so that it cannot respond to legitimate traffic.

Dial-up: The ability of a remote user to access a system by using private or common carrier telephone lines.

Digital Certification: A process to authenticate (or certify) a party's digital signature, carried out by trusted third parties.

Digital Signature: A mathematical encryption technique that associates a specific person with a given computer file and indicates that the file has not been altered since that person signed it. It should not be confused with making an electronic representation of a written signature.

Digital: Referring to communications processors, techniques, and equipment where information is encoded as a binary "1" or "0".

Distributed Transaction Processing: Application processing that involves multiple users requiring concurrent access to a single shared resource.

Domain Name: An alphanumeric name for a web site that includes both the online address and online name.

DOS: Disk operating system.

Download: To transmit a file or programme from a central computer to a smaller computer or a remote site.

Electronic Cash: The digital equivalent of dollar or some other currency unit (also referred to as digital cash).

Electronic Data Interchange (EDI): The transfer of information between organizations in machine-readable form.

Electronic Document: The digital or computer equivalent of paper documents.

Electronic Money: Monetary value measured in currency units stored in electronic form on an electronic device in the consumer's possession. This electronic value can be purchased and held on the device until reduced through purchase or transfer.

Electronic Purse: A stored value device that can be used to make purchases from more than one vendor.

E-mail: Messages people send to one another electronically from one computer to another.

Encryption (Cryptography): The process of scrambling data by a device or encoding principle (mathematical algorithms) so that the data cannot be read without the proper codes for unscrambling the data.

End-to-end Encryption: The protection of information passed in a telecommunications system by cryptographic means, from point of origin to point of destination.

Ethernet: A type of local area network originally developed by Xerox, communication takes place by means of radio frequency signals carried over coaxial cable.

File Transfer Protocol (FTP): A standard way of transferring files from one computer to another on the Internet.

Firewall: A system or combination of hardware and software solutions that enforces a boundary between two or more networks.

Flowchart: A programming tool to graphically present a procedure by using symbols to designate the logic of how a problem is solved.

Gateway: A computer that performs protocol conversion between different types of networks or applications.

Giga byte (GB): It means 1 billion (million x 1,000) bytes.

Graphical User Interface (GUI): A way of communicating with a computer by manipulating icons (pictures) and windows with a mouse.

Groupware: Software that allows a group of people to work on the same data through a network, by facilitating file sharing and other forms of communication.

Hacker: A computer operator who breaks into a computer without authorization, either for malicious reasons or just to prove it can be done.

Hacking: It refers to the practice of breaking into a computer without authorisation, for malicious reasons, just to prove it can be done, or for other personal reasons.

Hard Disk (HD): It is computer's storage space. HDs are measured in mega bytes/giga bytes.

HDD: Hard Disk Drive.

Home Banking: Banking services that allow a customer to interact with a financial institution from a remote location by using a telephone, television set, terminal, personal computer, or other device to access a telecommunication system which links to the institution's computer centre.

Home Page: A screen of information made available to users through the Internet or a private intranet; it is the "main page" that users are expected to read first in order to access the other pages that comprise the web site.

Host Computer: It is the primary or controlling computer in a computer network, generally involving data communications or a local area network.

Hypertext Mark-up Language (HTML): A set of codes that can be inserted into text files to indicate special typefaces, inserted images, and links to other hypertext documents.

Hypertext Transfer Protocol (HTTP): A standard method of publishing information as hypertext in HTML format on the Internet.

Hypertext: Electronic documents that present information which can be connected together in many different ways, instead of sequentially.

Identification: It is concerned with positively establishing the identity of the person or organisation conducting the transaction. Passwords are a common approach although evolving approaches such as biometrics may become increasingly prevalent. Authorisation is concerned with establishing the authority that an individual has to conduct a particular transaction.

Incident Response Team: A team of computer experts (internal or external) organized to protect an organization's data, systems, and other assets from attack by hackers, viruses etc.

Indent: Space left at the beginning of a line of print.

Integrated Circuit Card (IC Card): A plastic card in which one or more integrated circuits are embedded (also called a chip card).

Internet Service Provider (ISP): An entity that provides access to the Internet and related services, generally for a fee.

Internet: A worldwide network of computer networks (commonly referred to as the Information Superhighway).

Interoperability: The compatibility of distinct applications, networks, or systems.

Intranet: A private network that uses the infrastructure and standards of the Internet and World Wide Web, but is cordoned off from the public Internet through firewall barriers.

Issuer: In a stored value or similar prepaid electronic money system, the entity which receives payment in exchange for value distributed in the system and which is obligated to pay or redeem transactions or balances presented to it.

Key: A secret value or code used in an encrypting algorithm known by one or both of the communicating parties.

Kilo bytes (KB): It means 1,000 bytes (characters).

Local Area Network (LAN): A network that connects several computers that are located nearby (in the same room or building), allowing them to share files and devices such as printers.

Lock and Key Protection System: A protection system that involves matching a key or password with a specific access requirement.

Logging: The storing of information about events that occurred on the firewall or network.

Magnetic Stripe: Used on debit, credit, and identification cards to store encoded information read by card readers; less secure than computer chip cards.

Mega bytes (MB): It means 1 million (10 lakh) bytes.

Mega hertz (MHz): It means mega cycle = 1 million hertz or cycles per second.

Memory Card: An integrated circuit (IC) card capable of storing information only.

Middleware: It is transaction-processing software that facilitates client/server communications over a network (e.g. TCP/IP) allowing client applications to access and update information from unlike platforms, databases and mainframes.

Multimedia: Audio and visual (music, pictures, graphics etc.).

Navigation: Moving through a complex system of menus/help files.

Network: A group of computers connected by cables or other means and using software that enables them to share equipment and exchange information. A system of software and hardware connected in a manner to support data transmission.

Node: Any device, including servers and workstations, connected to a network. Also, the point where devices are connected.

Non-repudiable Transactions: Transactions that cannot be denied after the fact.

Off-line: Equipment or devices that are not in direct communication with the central processor of a computer system, or connected only intermittently.

On-line Scrip: Debit accounts on the Internet or other major computer network.

On-line Service Providers (OSP): Closed network services that provide access to various computer sites or networks for a fee.

On-line: Equipment or devices that communicate with a computer network. Connections can be direct (as in a LAN using dedicated connections) or indirect (as in using the Internet).

Open Network: A telecommunications network to which access is not restricted.

Open Stored Value System: A system that may be comprised of one or more electronic cash issuers of stored value which is accepted by multiple merchants or entities.

Operating System: A programme that controls a computer and makes it possible for users to enter and run their own programmes.

Package: A package consists of modules. The two popular modules in MS office are: (a) MS Word for word processing, and (b) MS Excel for data processing.

Packet Switching: A data transmission method that routes packets along the most efficient path and allows a communication channel to be shared by multiple connections.

Password Cracker: A software programme designed to conduct an automated brute force attack on the password security controls of an information system by *guessing* user passwords.

Password Sniffer: A software programme that is illicitly inserted somewhere on a network to capture user passwords as they pass through the system.

Password: A unique word or string of characters that a programmer, computer operator, or user must supply to satisfy security requirements before gaining access to the system or data.

Payment System: A financial system that establishes the means for transferring money between suppliers and users of funds, usually by exchanging debits or credits between financial institutions.

Personal Identification Number (PIN): A sequence of digits used to verify the identity of a device holder.

Piggyback (Between-the-lines Entry): A means of gaining unauthorized access to a system via another user's legitimate connection.

Point of Sale (POS): A system of terminals that debits or charges a customer's account and credits or pays a merchant's account to effect payment for purchases at retail establishments.

Port: Connection for printer.

Prepaid Card: A card on which value is stored, and for which the holder has paid the issuer in advance.

Privacy: In the context of a payment system, the property that no information which might permit determination of transactions may be collected without the consent of the counterparties involved.

Protocols: A standardized set of rules that define how computers communicate with each other.

Proximity Cards: Cards which can be read from a short distance; mainly used for security and vehicle identification.

Random Access Memory (RAM): Current memory as against stored memory on the hard disk.

Remote Payment: A payment carried out through the sending of payment orders or payment instruments.

Repudiation: The denial by one of the parties to a transaction of participation in all or part of that transaction or of the content of the communication.

Router: A computer system in a network which stores and forwards data packets between local area networks and wide area networks.

Scattering: The process of mixing the integrated circuit (IC) chip components so that they cannot be analyzed easily.

Search Engines: Software programmes which are capable of locating specified information or web sites on the Internet.

Secure Electronic Transaction (SET): A set of standards jointly developed by Visa, MasterCard, and several technologies companies to facilitate secure credit card transactions over the Internet.

Secure Socket Layer (SSL): A protocol for providing data security during transmission using data encryption, server authentication, and message integrity.

Server: A computer that provides services to another computer (the client).

Settlement System: A system used to facilitate the settlement of transfers of funds.

Settlement: An act that discharges obligations with respect to funds or securities transfers between two or more parties.

Simple Mail Transfer Protocol (SMTP): A protocol used to transfer electronic mail between computers on the Internet.

Smart Card: A card with a computer chip embedded, on which financial, health, educational, and security information can be stored and processed.

Sniffing: It involves the use of a software programme which is illicitly inserted somewhere on a network to capture (*sniff*) user passwords as they pass through the system.

Special Video Graphics Adapter (SVGA): Used for quick display of graphics.

Specification: Documents that contain basic detailed data.

Spoofing: It refers to an attempt to gain access to a system by posing as an authorised user.

Standards: The rules under which analysts, programmers, operators, and other personnel in an information service organization work.

Stored Value Card: A card which stores prepaid value via magnetic stripe or computer chip.

Straight-through Processing: It refers to automatic transaction processing without any human intervention in the transaction process flow.

Structured Query Language (SQL): A query language used to manipulate large databases.

System Integrity: The quality that a system has when it performs its intended function in an unimpaired manner, free from deliberate or inadvertent manipulation of the system.

System Specification: A baseline specification containing all the essential computer-based business system documentation. It is completed at the end of the development phase.

Systemic Risk: The risk that the failure of one participant in a funds transfer system to meet its required obligations will cause other participants to be unable to meet their obligations when due.

Systems Analysis: The performance, management, and documentation of the four phases of the life cycle of a business system: study, design, development, and operation.

Tamper-evident: The capacity of devices to show evidence of physical attack.

Tamper-proof: The proven capacity of devices to resist all attacks.

Tamper-resistant: The capacity of devices to resist physical attack up to a certain point.

Telecommunications: Data transmission between a computing system and remotely located devices via telephone lines, cable, or wireless technology.

Telnet: A protocol which permits users to access a remote terminal or another computer through a network; widely used on the Internet.

Threat Monitoring: The analysis, assessment, and review of audit trails and other data collected for the purpose of searching out system events which may constitute violations or attempted violations of system security.

Throughput: The total amount of useful work performed by a data processing system during a given period of time.

Traceability: The degree to which transactions can be traced to the originator or recipient (also referred to as auditability).

Transferability: In electronic money systems, the degree to which an electronic balance can be transferred between devices without interaction with a central authority.

Transmission Control Protocol (TCP)/Internet Protocol (IP): A standard format for transmitting data in packets from one computer to another, on the Internet and within other networks. TCP deals with the construction of the data packets while IP routes them from machine to machine.

Trap Door: A concealed and unauthorized entrance into a computer operating system, designed by the programmer.

Trojan Horse: A programme which appears to perform a useful function and sometimes does so quite well but also includes an unadvertised feature, which is usually malicious in nature.

Truncation: Dropping off part of a character string either to conserve space or because of limited space.

Trusted Computer System: A system that employs sufficient assurance measures to allow its use for simultaneous processing of a range of sensitive or classified information.

Trusted Third Party: A reputable entity that authenticates one or more parties to an electronic transaction. The authentication process generally involves the issuance and administration of digital certificates.

Uniform Resource Locator or Universal Resource Locator (URL): A way of specifying the location of available information on the Internet.

Upload: To transmit a file to a central computer from a smaller computer or a remote location.

Usenet: A set of many newsgroups distributed via the Internet.

VDU: Visual Display Unit.

Virtual Corporations: Corporations that have no official physical site presence and are made up of diverse geographically dispersed or mobile employees.

Virus: A programme with the ability to reproduce by modifying other programmes to include a copy of itself. It may contain destructive code that can move into multiple programmes, data files, or devices on a system and spread through multiple systems in a network.

Vulnerability: A weakness in system security procedures, system design, implementation, internal controls etc. which could be exploited to violate system security.

Web Page: A screen of information supporting the home page of a web site.

Web Site: The collection of an entity's home page and other proprietary pages located on the World Wide Web.

Wide Area Network (WAN): A communications network that covers a wide geographic area, such as state or country, using high speed long distance lines or satellites provided by a common carrier.

World Wide Web (web, www): A sub network of the Internet through which information is exchanged via text, graphics, audio, and video.

Worm: A programme that scans a system or an entire network for available, unused space in which to run. Worms tend to tie up all computing resources in a system or on a network and effectively shut it down.

XML: XML (Extensible Mark-up Language) is a universal, flexible, text-based data format which facilitates structured data interchange on the Web.